BRITAIN IN OLD PHOTOGRAPHS

THEATRICAL LONDON

PATRICIA DEE BERRY

ALAN SUTTON PUBLISHING LIMITED

Alan Sutton Publishing Limited
Phoenix Mill · Far Thrupp · Stroud
Gloucestershire · GL5 2BU

First published 1995

Copyright © Patricia Dee Berry, 1995

Cover photograph: (front) The Arcadians,
with Mr Dan Rolyat as 'James Smith';
(back) the cast of *Richard III*.

British Library Cataloguing in Publication Data.
A catalogue record for this book is available from
the British Library.

ISBN 0-7509-0942-0

Typeset in 9/10 Sabon.
Typesetting and origination by
Alan Sutton Publishing Limited.
Printed in Great Britain by
Hartnolls, Bodmin, Cornwall.

Contents

Introduction

For centuries the world of the play-actor has fascinated its audiences. Long ago the stark routine of many a village community was only relieved on the brief joyous occasions when some company of players came along. The comparative glamour of new faces, bright colours and strange dialogue must have had a dazzling effect on the unsophisticated spectators: small wonder that the young and impressionable were tempted to leave home and take to the road with the players when they moved on. Small wonder, too, that the itinerant nature of actors' existence had them officially classed as 'rogues and vagabonds', with the women thought 'no better than they should be'.

Yet this was the way in which some of our earlier leading players began; no Royal Academy of Dramatic Art, no Italia Conti school, no agents to start them off. In researching the lives of some of these greats, I have found time and again that they achieved recognition on the London stage after years of provincial struggle. Writers including Charles Dickens, Thomas Hardy and J.B. Priestley used such experiences in some of their stories.

London was the ultimate goal for most old-time actors, though only a small proportion achieved this. From late Tudor times, places like The Theatre, the Curtain, the Rose, the Swan, the Fortune and, best-known, the oft-quoted 'wooden O' of Shakespeare's Globe, were being built for the entertainment of the people and the prestige of the playwrights.

Seventeenth- and eighteenth-century royal patronage went some way towards making the acting profession respectable, blighted by a decade of Puritan embargo. The Theatres Royal of Drury Lane, Covent Garden and the Haymarket survive for us today, built and licensed more than two hundred years ago. Several theatres are the third or even fourth on the same site, often because of earlier loss by fire. The Globe itself burned down in 1613 and, right up to the advent of electric power, it was candleflame, pyrotechnic effects and naked footlights that were responsible for a number of conflagrations. (As late as 1951, John Gielgud commented on the combustibility of his family, after his cousin, Hazel Terry, accidentally set light to herself during *A Winter's Tale* at the Phoenix.)

This is essentially a book of old photographs, but it would not do to tell stories of the London theatre without reference to its founding fathers and the buildings in which they worked in pre-photography days. I have, therefore, cheated a little by showing some ancient prints and paintings, and even a statue or two. The small print in old programmes sometimes gives unfamiliar guidance to patrons, such as the prohibition of bonnets, or what to do in an air-raid, and so one or two programmes are reproduced too.

The invention of the camera and the picture postcard did much to publicize Victorian players, and no doubt the opportunity to 'put a voice to a face' inspired many would-be playgoers to venture into a London theatre. The careers of Ellen Terry, Henry Irving, Herbert Tree, John Hare and George Alexander were among the first to be affected in this way, followed, in the Edwardian era, by the actor–managers Martin-Harvey, Forbes-Robertson, Benson, Waller, Maude and Granville-Barker.

The search for photographs for my collection has taken me to collectors' and antiques fairs and shops, from which it has become clear that glamour photography is nothing new. The Dare sisters Zena and Phyllis, Gladys Cooper, Constance Collier, Ellaline Terriss, Pauline Chase and other beauties were interminably pictured in improbable costumes and settings. It is obvious from the messages written on the postcards – 'Here's another for your album', or 'Hope you don't already have this one of your favourite' – that these ladies had admirers everywhere.

A life-long passion for the theatre was encouraged by my parents; our house, like many others, had special catch-phrases culled from favourite plays: 'The bells! The bells!', 'Not even for ready money', 'Say you believe in fairies', 'District Nurse!!'.* I began with an interest in Ellen Terry whose photographs formed the nucleus of my collection. For the past 14 years I have had the immense pleasure and privilege through association with the Theatregoers' Club of Great Britain of seeing some of the best plays in the loveliest theatres in London.

Standing in the foyer of any of these buildings, taking a seat in the auditorium where countless thousands have cheered (and some hissed), seeing the house lights dim (a practice introduced only 120 years ago), and awaiting yet another performance on a stage trodden by players great and small, past and present, success and flop: I hope in these pages to share all these pleasures with readers. Through my work, opportunities have also arisen to join backstage guided tours and to meet some of our leading actors. They have talked about traditions, superstitions and anecdotes of that other world, separated from reality by footlights and a curtain – sometimes, these days, implied but invisible.

In the rush and roar of arrival at the theatre, leaving one's coat, buying a programme, finding one's seat, it is easy to ignore the history all around and forget the subtle changes that have taken place within the time limits of this book. Curtain calls used to be taken at the end of each act of a play; all first-circle patrons were expected to wear formal dress (hence 'dress circle'); the main play was often preceded by a 'curtain-raiser'; and an evening's entertainment often began at 8.30 pm, with 'carriages at eleven'.

Modern life is frequently touched by the theatre, from the actors seen on film and television, their very-public private lives, to the phrases we use such as 'up-staging' someone, 'hogging the limelight', 'play the heavy father', 'up in the gods' and 'a stage-whisper'.

* From *The Bells*, *The Importance of Being Earnest*, *Peter Pan* and *Dear Octopus* respectively; the last phrase was used as a children's 'swearword'.

If readers of this book do not find their favourite play, theatre or player mentioned, I beg them to remember that the pictures included are from my personal collection which does not cover the whole field. Though the book is about theatrical London, I make no apology for a number of references to the more recent entertainment media of cinema and television. Well over half the principal players shown herein also appeared on film, which is the only way their talents can be judged today. Sadly, the grand gestures and measured diction necessary on an Edwardian stage did not always transfer to the intimacy of the movie camera, with occasional unhappy results.

The royal box at the London Coliseum.

Section One

DRURY LANE & ALDWYCH

Theatre Royal, Drury Lane. The oldest surviving London
theatre, this fourth building on the site opened in 1812.
The original was granted a charter by Charles II 150 years
earlier, in the days when only the Patent Theatres (this and
Covent Garden) were permitted to stage straight drama.
Parts of the second theatre on the site, designed by
Christopher Wren in 1674, still stand, though hidden.

Statue of Mrs Sarah Siddons (1755–1831) at Paddington Green. One of the famous theatrical Kemble family – her brothers were John Philip, Stephen and Charles – from childhood she acted in her father Roger's travelling company. Her first venture at Drury Lane, at the age of 20 (two years after her marriage to fellow actor William Siddons) was a failure, but her return in 1782, at the invitation of manager Richard Brinsley Sheridan, was a triumph. It was during her time at Drury Lane that actor Robert Baddeley's bequest came into effect: his £100 at 3 per cent has provided the resident cast with cake and rum punch every Twelfth Night since 1794.

Ira Aldridge (1804–67). A bust of this respected black American actor is displayed in the upper circle rotunda of the Theatre Royal. After appearing in New York he came to London to play Othello at the age of 22. Thereafter he acted in London and on the continent in Shakespearean roles, including Lear, for which he wore white make-up. His daughter, also Ira, worked with another black actor, Paul Robeson, in preparing his portrayal of 'the noble Moor' at the Savoy Theatre in 1930, with Peggy Ashcroft as his Desdemona.

Memorial card for Henry Irving (1838–1905). Although the Lyceum (p. 19) had been the setting for his greatest dramatic triumphs over a period of almost 30 years, Irving was last at the Theatre Royal from 1903 to 1905. The first actor to be knighted (in 1895), his 24-year stage partnership with Ellen Terry in London and the provinces, and on tour in Canada and America, brought high-quality productions to many thousands of playgoers.

John L. Toole (1830–1906). Toole was 26 when he first appeared in London, after four years in the provinces. He acted with Henry Irving, and in adaptations of novels by Charles Dickens – both became his lifelong friends. In 1882, after some years at the Gaiety, he reopened at Toole's Theatre, a converted hall in King William Street previously called the Charing Cross and also the Folly. A number of actors featured in this book had their start at Toole's, which was demolished in 1896 to make way for an extension to the then Charing Cross Hospital.

A JUBILEE SOUVENIR of England's Greatest Actress 1856-1906

MISS ELLEN TERRY (ABOUT 40 YEARS AGO)

Women will love her that she is a woman More worthy than any man: men, that She is the rarest of all women.
The Winter's Tale, Shakespeare

Ellen Terry jubilee, 12 June 1906. On 28 April 1856 nine-year-old 'Nelly', fifth child of travelling players Ben and Sarah Terry, first appeared on stage at the Princess's, Oxford Street (p. 152) as Mamillius in Charles Kean's production of *The Winter's Tale*. A few months later, rising on the wooden stage lift for her final speech as Puck in *A Midsummer Night's Dream*, she suffered agonies when her toe was crushed between trap and floor. She was promised double salary by Mrs Kean, who rushed to the rescue, and thus the little girl played on. The rest of her distinguished acting career was just as colourful, courageous and eventful. Despite her belief that 'nobody will remember', her 50 years on the stage were celebrated with a banquet and a five-hour matinée at Drury Lane. It benefited Ellen by over £6,000 with a further £3,000 from an affectionate public's Jubilee Celebration Fund. All the leading actors of the day appeared, including the French leading lady Réjane (left) and over 20 members of Ellen's family, but not great-nephew John Gielgud (p. 63), then only two years old.

Dan Leno (George Galvin) (1860–1904).
Contortionist, clog-dancer, Cockney singer,
music-hall comedian, comic paper hero,
pantomime dame: from 'Little George' at the
age of four, Dan Leno was an entertainer all
his life. For 16 years, until his death in a
mental hospital following a nervous
breakdown, he appeared in the Christmas
pantomime at Drury Lane, where his carved
likeness can be seen to this day. Widow
Twanky, Dame Trot and Mother Goose were
favourite roles. In 1901 the new King
Edward VII summoned him to perform at
Sandringham.

Harry Randall (1860–1932). Another
popular comedian, Harry Randall began
specializing in dame roles in 1893 as
Mother Hubbard. He played alongside
Dan Leno in the latter's last appearance in
Humpty Dumpty at Drury Lane in 1903,
and then succeeded to the dame part. He is
remembered to this day in rhyming slang,
his name being a substitute for 'handle'.

Frank Benson (1858–1939). Frank Benson (above right, as Richard III) differed from some of the other Edwardian actor-managers in coming from a well-to-do family and receiving a university education. While at New College Oxford he was prominent in both athletics and drama. At 24 he was engaged by Irving to play Paris in *Romeo and Juliet* at the Lyceum, and the following year founded the F.R. Benson Company with which he toured the country for the rest of his life, including 30 years of seasons at the Shakespeare Memorial Theatre in Stratford-upon-Avon (below). After the Shakespeare Tercentenary performance of *Julius Caesar* at Drury Lane in 1916, Benson was summoned to the retiring room behind the royal box, where he was knighted by George V, who dubbed him with a sword from the property room.

Scenes from *The Garden of Allah*, 1920. The play was adapted by Robert Hichens from his own novel in collaboration with Mary Anderson, and had already played New York before it was produced at Drury Lane, with music by Landon Ronald. Later it transferred to the cinema with Charles Boyer and Marlene Dietrich. Above, left to right in the foreground, are Harry Ludlow, Madge Titheradge, Basil Gill, Godfrey Tearle and Arthur Lewis. The cast also included a number of donkeys, sheep, camels and other animals that gave authenticity to scenes like the market and the oasis (below). An impressive desert storm was created by having fine meal blown around the stage by electric fans. On the first night the audience seated in the front stalls were covered in dust because a protective see-through curtain had not been lowered. All was well, however, by 1 July, when the play was performed in the presence of George V.

Noël Coward (1899–1973). The tradition of presenting musicals at Drury Lane began on 20 March 1925 with *Rose Marie* (which ran for 851 performances). Six years later, actor-playwright Noël Coward, who had already produced a number of successful plays, revues and operettas, wrote a spectacular musical play, *Cavalcade*, for C.B. Cochran, at the Coliseum.

Cavalcade was eventually produced at Drury Lane with Mary Clare (inset, right) portraying Jane Marryot, around whom the 30-year family story revolves. The cast of 250 included real soldiers who swelled the ranks for the troopship scene. It was subsequently filmed with Diana Wynyard and Clive Brook, and was received as a patriotic appeal to the nation in the unsettled twenties, a 'call to arms' which the author had not exactly intended.

Ivor Novello (1893–1951) and *Crest of the Wave*. Ivor Novello came from a family of musicians and as a boy moved among stage and concert personalities; he was a pageboy at the wedding of Beatrice Stella Tanner (Mrs Patrick Campbell). When only 21 he wrote a popular First World War song (p. 126); in the 1920s he became a matinée idol of silent movies, he appeared on stage for *Deborau* in 1921 and thereafter composed plays in which he acted. *Crest of the Wave* was presented at Drury Lane and included a spectacular train crash scene and the first-act number (below) entitled 'Nautical'. The one and only coalition of the remarkable talents of Ivor Novello and Noël Coward was in 1927 when the first night of Coward's *Sirocco* at Daly's with Novello and Frances Doble (p. 41) as the romantic leads, was a disaster: the play closed after 28 performances.

Lionel Brough (1836–1900). Although he became famous in later life for his comic roles at the Gaiety and with Tree at Her Majesty's, this actor's first London appearance was at Covent Garden in one of his older brother William's plays. Lionel's son Sydney, daughter Mary and niece Fanny (daughter of another brother Robert) all excelled in comedy.

Royal Opera House, Covent Garden, c. 1890. The second of the true Theatres Royal, with King George II's charter dating from 1732, the present building is the third on the site, which had once been the garden of a convent. Both earlier buildings were destroyed by fire. The first was in 1808, when the building where child prodigy Master William Betty had played was lost and 20 firemen died. The second fire was in 1856. On this occasion the flames ruined the theatre where the great Edmund Kean, as Othello, had fallen dying into the arms of his son Charles.

The Fortune, 1927: Tom Walls. This small theatre in Russell Street, on the site of the old Albion inn, was the first built after the end of the First World War, in 1924, in the then fashionable Art Deco style; a statue of Terpsichore, the muse of dance, stands high above the entrance. The Sean O'Casey plays *Juno and the Paycock* and *The Plough and the Stars* were presented here in 1926, after which Tom Walls, from the Aldwych farces (p. 31) took over and presented Lonsdale's *On Approval*. By 1932, the year his horse April the Fifth won the Epsom Derby, Tom Walls had parted company with the Fortune.

The Dark Saint, Fortune, 1932. After Tom Walls came Nancy Price and her People's National Theatre 'created and maintained voluntarily by the public rather than state supported'. Next, Sybil Thorndike, who studied with Sir Ben Greet's company (p. 155), appeared in several roles. In this scene with Catherine Lacey, she is seated on the right.

The Fortune. From the mid-1930s until the outbreak of the Second World War (during which it was occupied by ENSA – Entertainments National Service Association), the Fortune was used by amateur companies for their productions (see also the Scala, p. 154). This scene from *The Mikado* is dated 30 May 1934, but the actors are unnamed.

Dirk Bogarde, 1947. In spite of a couple of promising young men in the cast, *Power without Glory*, an early post-war drama, had little chance of success in competition with *Oklahoma!* at the Theatre Royal opposite. The young actors were Kenneth More and Dirk Bogarde. *At the Drop of a Hat* (Flanders and Swann, 1956), *Beyond the Fringe* (Miller, Bennett, Cook and Moore, 1961) and *The Woman in Black* (from Susan Hill's novel, 1988 and into the 1990s) are among the theatre's post-war successes.

The Lyceum, Wellington Street, c. 1850. This was the third theatre on or very near the same site, and was the one in which Ellen Terry and Henry Irving acted together every year between 1871 and 1902; he was the lessee for almost all that time. 'Lyceum' can mean 'lecture hall' or 'talking place', and the original building (1765–1812) was intended as a concert hall, exhibition- and lecture-rooms. In 1904 the Lyceum was rebuilt to Bertie Crewe's design; very little remained of the theatre Irving knew, except the portico (still there today) around whose pillars black bands were draped after his death on 13 October 1905.

Ellen Terry as Beatrice in *Much Ado about Nothing*, 1880. Ellen Terry also played this role on tour with her second husband, Charles Kelly, and was able to repeat it in the next Lyceum season, to great acclaim. She was 35, reacting to the critics' dislike (though popular success) of *Romeo and Juliet*, with Irving at 44 playing the young hero. Her daughter Edy thought her mother was wrong to put her hair in a fringe! The photograph shows all the warmth and fun of the real Ellen, so often repressed for her solemn or tragic roles.

Revival of *Olivia*, 1885. This was originally produced at the Royal Court (p. 61) in 1878, with William Terriss (p. 43) and Ellen's children, Edward and Edy, in the cast. The Lyceum revival, however, with Irving as 'Doctor Primrose' (the vicar of Wakefield and Olivia's father) was well received. Ellen's costumes inspired a fashion in 'Olivia bonnets' and 'Olivia scarves' among the young female population.

Italia Conti (1874–1946). Miss Conti appeared at the Lyceum in 1891 in Augustus Daly's production of *The Last Word* (in which the American actress Ada Rehan starred). After many years with touring companies in England and Australia, in 1911 Italia was invited by Charles Hawtrey to train the cast of some 50 children (including Master Noël Coward) for the new Christmas play *Where the Rainbow Ends*, which thereafter was presented annually. Her stage school was founded the same year and acknowledgements like 'pupils of Italia Conti' or 'by arrangement with Italia Conti' can often be found in my collection of programmes for plays ranging from *The Miracle* and *Autumn Crocus* (both 1932) to *Peter Pan* (1951).

The Passing of the Third Floor Back. Another knighted actor-manager of the Edwardian era was Johnston Forbes-Robertson (1853–1937), who would rather have been a painter. After some coaching from the old Shakespearian Samuel Phelps, he played in the London and provincial companies of Irving, the Bancrofts (p. 68) and John Hare (p. 86), and did three autumn seasons at the Lyceum, while Irving toured. Jerome K. Jerome's 'mystical parable' *The Passing of the Third Floor Back* (1908 at the St James's) was Forbes-Robertson's greatest box-office success. He married Gertrude Elliott (right).

Carl Rosa Opera Company. Carl August Nicolas Rosa (really Rose), born in Hamburg in 1842, was involved with music and singing all his life. He presented his operatic company at the Prince's in 1875, and from 1893 was able to attach 'Royal' to their name, following a command performance before Queen Victoria at Balmoral. Their annual seasons in London included appearances at the Lyceum in 1898, 1919, 1925, 1929 and 1935.

John Martin-Harvey (1863–1944). Martin-Harvey (left) entered Irving's company at the Lyceum in 1882. Encouraged by his wife Nina de Silva (right), in 1899 he went into management for himself with *The Only Way*, an adaptation of Dickens' *A Tale of Two Cities*, presented at the Lyceum and transferring to the Prince of Wales. He was knighted in 1921 and continued to play 'Sydney Carton' (his admiring public's favourite) till the age of 76.

William Gillette (1855–1937) as Sherlock Holmes. In September 1901 this American actor brought his interpretation of the Conan Doyle character to the Lyceum. It is said that the eccentric costumes, meerschaum pipe and other items associated today with the great detective were developed by Gillette, based on the original *Strand Magazine* illustrations. Gillette built himself a fantastic home in the United States, where Sherlock Holmes devotees convene to this day. He also starred in his own adventure/mystery plays such as *Secret Service*. He retired from the stage at 77.

Playwright Thomas Henry Hall Caine. *The Prodigal Son* (1905) advertised at Drury Lane (p. 7) was one of this writer's religious plays adapted from his own novel and performed there and at the Lyceum. *The Christian* was another, and *Pete* (see next page) was an adaptation of an earlier play *The Manxman*. Hall Caine was himself from the Isle of Man, and a friend of the Pre-Raphaelite poet and painter Dante Gabriel Rossetti.

Matheson Lang in *Pete*. Alexander Matheson Lang (1879–1948) came from Canada at 18, later joining Benson's company (p. 12). After a time at the Royal Court, his reputation was established with a Lyceum revival of *The Christian* in 1907, and he appeared as 'Pete' some two years later. He formed his own touring company and acted with his wife Hutin Britton in *The Good Hope* and other plays.

Diaghilev and his Ballets Russes. Sergei Pavlovich de Diaghilev (1872–1929) (second from left) arrived on the ballet scene in 1909 by way of music lessons with Rimsky-Korsakov, promoting art exhibitions in St Petersburg, and concerts and opera in Paris. He gathered together a brilliant touring company dancing to music, dressed in costumes, amid scenery, all of Russian origin. The company made a number of visits to London, with a sell-out season at the Lyceum three years before Diaghilev's death.

The Melville era. The Lyceum, rebuilt in 1904, continued to detour from Shakespeare via music-hall and plays to popular melodrama and pantomime. Brothers Frederick, Walter and Andrew Melville were fifth-generation theatricals who shared some £100,000 under their father's will. While Andrew pursued a successful career in Brighton, the other two began a 25-year tenure of the Lyceum. They wrote their own scripts and kept loyal audiences and players year after year.

Pearl White. The star of long-running silent movie serials from America like *The Perils of Pauline* and *The Exploits of Elaine*, 'dare-devil heroine' Pearl White visited England in 1925. She appeared in a Lyceum show *The London Revue*, where Jack Hylton and his band played the music. It may have disappointed her admirers, as it is reported that she did not once fall down a raging torrent or escape from a burning building in all 77 performances.

The Miracle. This religious spectacle, directed by Austrian Max Reinhardt, was presented by Charles B. Cochran in the great arena of Olympia, West London, in 1912 (above) and revived 20 years later at the Lyceum, with Humperdinck's music and Oliver Messel's costumes. Not only the stage but also the auditorium was decorated to resemble a Gothic cathedral, hence (see programme announcement below), the customary interval teas could not be brought to playgoers in their seats.

Lottie Venne (1852–1928) in *The Rivals*, *c.* 1910. This veteran actress, seen far left as Mrs Malaprop with Lewis Waller as Captain Absolute, provides a link with the original Strand theatre, which stood for over 70 years at the eastern end of the Strand until it was demolished in 1905. Part of Aldwych underground station now occupies the site. Miss Venne played at the theatre during one of its happier interludes when light opera and burlesque were presented. At other times the old Strand's fortunes sank very low.

Louie Freear (?1872–1939). The last success at the old Strand was *A Chinese Honeymoon* (1901) with Lily Elsie (p. 121) and J. Farren Soutar as the romantic leads and Louie Freear giving a 'droll' performance as 'Fifi'. Earlier, she had worked with Ben Greet (p. 155) and as 'Puck' with Herbert Tree in *A Midsummer Night's Dream*.

W. Clarkson advertisement, 1901. Wellington Street, off the Strand, housed not only the Lyceum but also Willy Clarkson's premises, patronized by many members of the London stage world. 'Wigs by Clarkson' appears in every one of my collection of Victorian and Edwardian programmes, where such acknowledgements are included (p. 140). This advertisement appeared at the back of the programme for *Sweet Nell of Old Drury*, which stated 'The wigs, armour, etc. by Mr William Clarkson'.

The Olympic, 6–10 Wych Street. Another theatre to disappear in the 1905 redevelopment of the Aldwych area was the Olympic. The first of three on the site was opened a century earlier by Philip Astley. It had a chequered history, being known at times as the Little Drury Lane Theatre, and only achieved success when the established actress Madame Vestris, excelling in singing and burlesque, became the first woman manager in London when she took over in 1830. Today we take for granted many of the reforms and innovations she brought in, such as the box (i.e. ceilinged) set, authentic costumes and properties. The second Olympic burned down and the last, erected in 1890, seated over 2,000.

The Winter Garden, 167 Drury Lane. Since the seventeenth century, a succession of buildings devoted to pleasure for the people has stood on this site. As a tavern, the Great Mogul, it was patronized by Nell Gwynne, and survived until Victorian times. A music hall, the Mogul Saloon ('the old Mo') was built alongside in 1847. In spite of renaming it the Middlesex Music Hall, and rebuilding in 1872, the nickname persisted. Further changes took place 39 years later when the New Middlesex Theatre of Varieties designed by Frank Matcham (p. 59) arose. Marie Lloyd (right), Dan Leno (p. 11) and many other entertainers appeared there. Not until 1919 was the music hall setting abolished, verbose 'chairman' and all, and yet another naming, as the Winter Garden, saw the theatre begin a 40-year career with *Kissing Time*, starring recently demobilized comedian Leslie Henson. In August 1927 it was further dignified when George V came to see *The Vagabond King*. After standing empty from 1959 until 1965, the Winter Garden was demolished and the New London (opening in 1973) rose on the site.

The Aldwych, looking west. Part of the curved terrace designed by W.G.R. Sprague for the grand redevelopment of an old slum area, the theatre named Aldwych opened at Christmas 1905 with a children's play presented by American impresario Charles Frohman (p. 100) and actor-manager Seymour Hicks (p. 135). In 1909 Chekhov's *The Cherry Orchard* had its disastrous first performance here; it was over 50 years before it returned, to great acclaim. For part of the First World War the theatre was used by the YMCA (Young Men's Christian Association) as a recreation hall for Australian troops.

The Gay Gordons, 1907. Written by Seymour Hicks and performed by him and his Falkland Islands-born wife Ellaline Terriss, this musical comedy was an early success for the Aldwych. Kneeling (centre) is Zena Dare who, like her equally beautiful sister Phyllis, graced many a glamour postcard of the era. Standing on the far right is Fred Emney Snr, who died tragically ten years later of injuries received during a slapstick pantomime scene. His son, also Fred (1900–80), was the larger-than-life comedian who enlivened many plays and films, well into his seventies.

Dirty Work, 1932. Ralph Lynn (left) and J. Robertson Hare were regular members of the 'Aldwych farce' team led by Tom Walls (p. 17), and including Mary Brough, daughter of Lionel (p. 16), Winifred Shotter and George Barrett. After *Tons of Money* (transferred from the Shaftesbury 1922) and *It Pays to Advertise* (1924), plays by Ben Travers such as *Cuckoo in the Nest, Rookery Nook* and *Thark*, filled the Aldwych for a decade.

The Waldorf Theatre, 1905. At the western end of Sprague's imposing Aldwych terrace, this theatre was ready in May 1905, seven months before its twin the Aldwych, with the Waldorf Hotel between them opening two years later. The posters advertise *Lights Out,* (below) an early production at the Waldorf with (left to right) Eva Moore, H.V. Esmond (her off-stage husband) and H.B. Irving (elder son of Henry).

The Strand, Waldorf Hotel, Aldwych, 1925. By this time, the Waldorf theatre had been called successively the Strand, the Whitney and (since 1913 and still today) the Strand. Ivor Novello, matinée idol and prolific composer of musical comedy (p. 15) made his London home in a flat at 11 Aldwych, above the theatre, for almost 40 years, until his death in 1951.

The Scarlet Pimpernel, 1915. Actor-manager Fred Terry, younger brother of Ellen, and his wife Julia Neilson, were appearing in a wartime revival of this old favourite, first presented in 1905, when a Zeppelin air-raid began. In costume as Sir Percy Blakeney, Fred went into the audience to reassure them, before proceeding with the play. History almost repeated itself in the Second World War when Donald Wolfit and his Shakespeare company had to rescue their costumes from bomb-damaged dressing-rooms before 'the show could go on'.

The Duchess, Catherine Street. A comparatively modern theatre with a mock-Tudor façade, the Duchess opened in 1929 and, within a year, had established a record – for the shortest run in history when *The Intimate Revue* closed before the end of the first performance. After some early presentations by Nancy Price's People's National Theatre and *Children in Uniform* starring 22-year-old Jessica Tandy (seated, left), playwright John Boynton Priestley brought his 'time-slip' plays here. In *Time and the Conways* (1937) were (below, left to right) Raymond Huntley, Jean Forbes-Robertson, Eileen Erskine, Barbara Everest, Rosemary Scott, Alexander Archdale, Helen Horsey, Molly Rankin and Wilfred Babbage. Mervyn Johns (father of Glynis, p. 104) completed the cast.

Section Two

THE STRAND & SOUTH

The Gaiety, at the junction of the Strand and Aldwych, 1935. In 1903 an earlier Gaiety theatre was another casualty in the grand redevelopment of Aldwych (p. 30). George Edwardes (The Guv'nor) staged musical comedies in the new Gaiety but after his death in 1915 its fortunes declined. Jack o' Diamonds *by Clifford Gray and H.F. Maltby with music by Noel Gay opened in February 1935. This was the year of George V and Queen Mary's silver jubilee, hence the bunting flying. For almost twenty years the Gaiety remained closed and derelict, until it was demolished in 1957 and the site redeveloped.*

The Spring Chicken c. 1905. Gertie Millar and Edmund Payne were the leading lady and chief comedian of several musical comedies at Edwardes' new Gaiety. One gathers that the story of *The Spring Chicken* concerned a guileless Englishman (played by Payne) and his adventures on holiday in Paris.

Our Miss Gibbs, 1909. Gertie Millar played 'Mary Gibbs', a shop assistant, while Edmund Payne was a trombonist from a prize-winning Yorkshire band, at one point mistaken for a marathon runner. Gertie introduced the evergreen song 'Moonstruck' ('I'm such a silly when the moon comes up . . . '). In this shop scene are Ruth Argent (centre), Gladys Homfrey (seated right) and Denise Orme (standing right). The posters in the background advertise the dancer Isadora Duncan (p. 76) and Pinero's play *The Gay Lord Quex*.

Gertie Millar and her first husband Lionel Monckton. Lionel Monckton went to university and studied for the bar but began writing for George Edwardes in 1901–2 with *A Country Girl* (at Daly's, p. 122). Gertie first sang his songs in *The Toreador* at the old Gaiety, then in *The Orchid*, in which newcomer Gabrielle Ray shocked audiences by appearing on stage in pink silk pyjamas. Monckton was also co-composer of *The Arcadians* (pp. 147–8). After his death in 1924, Gertie, the daughter of a mill-worker from Bradford, married the Earl of Dudley.

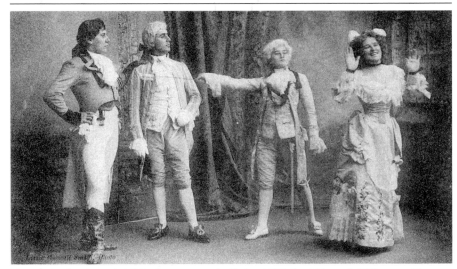

Terry's in the Strand. This theatre was built in 1887 for Edward O'Connor Terry, a former star of the old Gaiety, and it had a great success with Pinero's *Sweet Lavender* the following year. *My Lady Molly* (above) by Sidney Jones did well there in 1903. Seen here, left to right: Richard Green, Walter Hyde, Sybil Arundale (p. 118), Decima Moore.

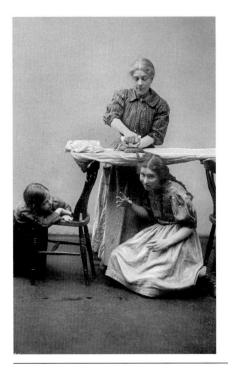

Mrs Wiggs of the Cabbage Patch was also successful in 1907, but Terry's closed three years later and was adapted as a cinema, the Grand Casino, which was demolished in 1923.

The Little, John Street, Adelphi. Seating only about 250, the theatre was formed from part of a bank in 1910. The following year Noël Coward (p. 14), aged eleven, made his London debut as Prince Mussel in a children's play *The Goldfish*. A Grand Guignol season (sensational and violent-actioned dramas) in 1920 featured Sybil Thorndike and her husband Lewis Casson.

Nancy Price took her People's National Theatre (p. 17) to the Little in the 1930s. The building suffered in air-raids in both world wars, and was damaged so badly in 1941 that it had to be demolished.

The Savoy. In 1907, John Eugene Vedrenne (left) with actor-manager Harley Granville-Barker moved from the Royal Court (p. 61) to impresario Richard D'Oyly Carte's riverside theatre, built to a design of C.J. Phipps, on a site close to the Chapel Royal and the old Savoy Palace. Advertised as the first public building to be lit entirely by electricity, it had opened in 1881 with Gilbert and Sullivan's *Patience*. Six more of their 'Savoy operas' had their first nights in the next eight years.

Harley Granville-Barker and Lillah McCarthy. Vedrenne and Granville-Barker continued to present plays at the Savoy but they could not repeat their earlier Royal Court success and parted company. After a few years Granville-Barker returned with memorable Shakespeare seasons that stunned audiences with sensationally simple sets and costumes by leading designer Norman Wilkinson, and the use of the full poetic texts. Lillah McCarthy (right), then Granville-Barker's wife, appeared as Viola in *Twelfth Night*, Hermione in *The Winter's Tale* and Helena in *A Midsummer Night's Dream*.

Paddy the Next Best Thing, 1920. This play was adapted from a successful novel by Gertrude Page, and ran at the Savoy for 867 performances before going on tour. It starred the popular Peggy O'Neil, who had a whisky named after her and many songs written about her. Five years later, she had another success in *Mercenary Mary* at the Hippodrome (p. 114), but failed in between at the Haymarket in *Plus Fours*, despite the fact that it was she who wore the golfing bloomers!

"If I miss that train I'll catch it!"

CECIL BARTH'S COMPANY By arrangement with ROBERT COURTNEIDGE

PADDY THE NEXT BEST THING

Young Woodley, 1928. John Van Druten's first play, set in a boys' school, was initially banned because it dealt with the touchy subject of an adolescent's love for his teacher's wife. The Council of the Stage Society (which promoted such outlawed works) took up the cause and gave Sunday performances of the play. It eventually opened at the Savoy and made a star of Frank Lawton (right) aged 24 as the schoolboy. Frances Doble and David Horne are also in the scene.

The Vaudeville. This theatre, which seats approximately 700, has stood on the same site in the Strand for 125 years. Since its creation by leading theatrical architect C.J. Phipps it has had two major reconstructions, and in 1895 Messrs Crompton and Company installed electrical heating. Between 1892 and 1969 it was owned by the famous Gatti brothers, restaurateurs and impresarios. Henry Irving had his big break on its stage, before moving to the Lyceum; Maude, Hawtrey, Frohman and Edwardes all spent some time there. The Hickses (p. 136) reigned for the first six years of the twentieth century, ending with *The Belle of Mayfair* in which Edna May and Charles Angelo (left) appeared. In 1911, two leading actresses were brought together when Sarah Bernhardt (right) played one of her breeches roles as 'Pelléas' to Mrs Patrick Campbell's 'Mélisande'.

The Adelphi. The 'Sans Pareil' ('Matchless') was built in 1806 for would-be star Jane Scott by her father, a wealthy merchant and inventor. Within 13 years it had changed hands and acquired the name we know today, though the proprietors had to wait until 1843 (with the lifting of the old Royal Charter embargo) to put on straight drama. A larger theatre was built in 1858.

William Terriss, 'Breezy Bill', father of Ellaline (Mrs Seymour Hicks), and one-time Irving player at the Lyceum, was admired for his good looks, virile acting and generous reputation. For more than a decade he played the hero in a series of 'Adelphi melodramas'. On Thursday 16 December 1897, as he stood at the entrance in Maiden Lane (built for Queen Victoria's last visit to the theatre in 1862), he was stabbed to death by Richard Arthur Prince, a member of his company who had an unfounded grudge against the star.

One of the Best: a drama of military life. Terriss appeared as 'Lieutenant Dudley Keppel of the Black Watch' in the 1895 production. In this postcard scene, however, where the hero is stripped of his military honours, the part is played by Henry Ainley, uttering the line, 'You may take my name, my honour, my life . . . but you cannot take my Victoria Cross!' The verdict, 'one of the worst', which Jerome K. Jerome's magazine *Today* attributed to 'a witty lady' is also ascribed to George Bernard Shaw. The play was written by George Edwardes (p. 117) and Seymour Hicks (p. 135).

The Quaker Girl, 1910. The team of George Edwardes, Lionel Monckton and Gertie Millar moved to the Adelphi for this musical comedy, which ran for more than 500 performances. In this scene, Gertie as 'Prudence' (centre) is with C. Hayden Coffin as 'Captain Charteris' a king's messenger, and Elsie Spain as 'Princess Mathilde', an exiled Bonapartist princess. Prudence's sweetheart, 'Tony Chute', Naval Attaché at the American Embassy in Paris ('Tony from America' in her song), was played by another Edwardes stalwart, Joseph Coyne. Even after the theatre was rebuilt in 1929, the luck held with shows having 'girl' in their title, with modern examples being *Charlie Girl* (over two thousand performances) and the revival of *Me and My Girl*.

The Adelphi, rebuilt for the third time, 1901. Only the outside walls and rear entrance of the old building were left in the reconstruction. Perhaps that is why there have been reported sightings of Breezy Bill's ghost wandering as far afield as Covent Garden underground station.

W.H. Berry. A comic who joined George Edwardes during his reign at Daly's in shows such as *Les Merveilleuses* and *The Merry Widow*, Berry went to the Adelphi for *The Naughty Princess*, *The Golden Moth*, *The Boy* (seen by George V in November 1918) and *Head over Heels* in 1923.

The Avenue (Playhouse). The first theatre on this corner site in Northumberland Avenue was put up in 1882, with the expectation that the land would soon be needed for the development of Charing Cross railway station, leading to compensation. This never happened, though the station was built very close by. However, in 1905, as rebuilding of the Avenue neared completion, part of the station collapsed and fell on to the theatre, killing six people and injuring a further 26. A sum of £20,000 was then paid in compensation and the Playhouse was built with a new interior behind the old façade. Its present charming decor and unusual arrangement of seating is the result of restoration after a long closure, except for a spell (1951–75) as a BBC studio from which the *Goon Show* and *Hancock's Half-Hour* were broadcast with live audiences.

C. Hayden Coffin. After an early appearance at the Avenue, in *Falka* (1885), this handsome singer was in demand for musical comedy. He played in *An Artist's Model, A Greek Slave, The Singalee, San Toy* and *A Country Girl*, all at Daly's (p. 116 *et seq*) and in *Tom Jones* (p. 133) at the Apollo in 1907. Five years later, Granville-Barker cast him as Feste in his production of *Twelfth Night* at the Savoy.

George Bernard Shaw (1856–1950). The Dublin-born playwright worked for many years as a critic of literature, art, music and drama, and had a brief spell as a novelist, before turning to stage writing. Three early plays were privately produced, and it was *Arms and the Man* that was first presented publicly, in April 1894 at the Avenue. *The Chocolate Soldier*, an operetta by Oscar Strauss, presented at the Lyric in 1910, was based on *Arms and the Man*, classified by Shaw himself as the first of his 'Plays Pleasant'.

The Flag Lieutenant, 1908. This play was billed as 'a naval comedy by Major W.P. Drury and Leo Trevor', and opened at the Avenue on 16 June 1908 running for 381 performances. It starred actor-manager Cyril Maude (far left) pictured with C. Aubrey Smith, who later went to Hollywood and specialized in military and patriarchal roles. I remember him as a magnificent 'Colonel Sapt' in *The Prisoner of Zenda,* and as the crusty grandfather of *Little Lord Fauntleroy.* Others in *The Flag Lieutenant* were Lilian Braithwaite and Mr Maude's wife Winifred Emery, and Lyonel Watts (seated) and Hugh Wakefield. Critic Sidney Drake in the *Green Room Book for 1908* enjoyed the show and commented 'good naval plays are rare'.

Bunty Pulls the Strings. Although it achieved its greatest success (617 performances) at the Theatre Royal, Haymarket, where George V saw it, this play was first put on in London at the Playhouse in 1911. Speaking in broad Scots, this large company (many from the same family) took the capital by storm. The young heroine 'Bunty Biggar' was played by Kate Moffat, while her brother Graham (the author) played 'Tammas Biggar'. The play was revived in 1913.

Gladys Cooper (1888–1971). An established actress and ubiquitous postcard beauty, Miss Cooper managed the Playhouse jointly with Frank Curzon in 1917; during 1927–33 she alone presented plays by Pinero, Lonsdale, Maugham and others. In this scene from *The Naughty Wife*, which opened in April 1918, she played 'Eloise Farrington' and her stage husband 'Hilary' was played by Charles Hawtrey (right). Her daughter Joan married actor Robert Morley, and their son is broadcaster, theatre critic and writer Sheridan Morley (named after 'Sheridan Whiteside' in *The Man Who Came to Dinner*, by Kaufman and Hart, 1941). Gladys was created Dame Commander of the British Empire in 1967.

Whiteoaks, 1938. In 1934 a young actor named Alec Guinness walked on at the Playhouse in *Libel* by Edward Wooll. For a year before the Second World War, Nancy Price and her People's National Theatre made the Playhouse their home. The adaptation of Mazo de la Roche's saga *Whiteoaks* – the family seen here with Miss Price as old Adeline Whiteoak ('Gran') at the head of the table – was one of their successes.

The Imperial (Aquarium). It can be seen that the theatrical centre of London moved westward over the years, from Bankside and the City in Elizabethan times by way of the Strand to the West End. A few theatres were built still farther west, but did not form any representative group, and some have not survived at all. The Imperial stood in Tothill Street, Westminster – where great Restoration actor Thomas Betterton was born – from 1876 to 1906; for a short time Lillie Langtry (p. 52) ran it, and in its dying years Ellen Terry, Lewis Waller and John Martin-Harvey all played here. On closure, it was taken down and rebuilt in Canning Town as the Imperial Palace Theatre. It became a cinema and burned down in 1931.

Mrs Lillie Langtry (1853–1929). Emilie Charlotte Le Breton was born in Jersey and was introduced to London society on her marriage to wealthy Edward Langtry. Her beauty and her reputation as a favourite of Edward, Prince of Wales (later Edward VII) gave 'the Jersey Lily' her entrée to the stage, where she first appeared in the Bancrofts' company (p. 68) at the Haymarket in 1881. She formed her own company, based at the Imperial, and toured with them here and in the United States.

Actors' Church Union funeral pall. Only yards from Tothill Street, in Westminster Abbey, on 11 November 1920 the Unknown Soldier was interred, a symbol of all who died in the First World War. The coffin was covered by this pall, presented to the Abbey by the Actors' Church Union in memory of all actors lost in the war. It is embroidered on white silk brocade with the Royal arms and those of the abbey, Saint Peter, Edward the Confessor and the Dean, with crowned Tudor roses and portcullis and the masks of Comedy and Tragedy with pan pipes, representing the acting profession.

Lewis Waller at the Imperial. Towards the end of an eventful career (from Toole's in 1883, at the age of 23, via provincial tours, Tree's company at the Haymarket and his own company at the Lyceum), Waller found the perfect play for his popular dashing style. *Monsieur Beaucaire* ran for 430 performances at the Comedy and became his stock revival. *Brigadier Gerard*, based on a story by Sir Arthur Conan Doyle (left) and presented during Waller's time at the Imperial (1906–10) gave him a similarly heroic part, but was not so well received by his droves of female admirers (the 'Keen On Waller' brigade!). Left to right in this scene from *Brigadier Gerard* (right) are Lewis Waller, Edward O'Neill and Evelyn Millard. *The Fires of Fate* was another Conan Doyle adaptation in which Lewis Waller played.

The St James's, King Street. This piece of theatrical history, where many great players had appeared, stood for more than 120 years with little rebuilding, though slightly bomb-damaged in 1944. It finally closed in 1957 prior to demolition, in spite of some highly charged protesting from actors and audiences. An office block now stands on the site.

As You Like It programme cover, 1897. This late Victorian programme design is one of the most attractive in my collection. Inside, a pencilled note records that 'F M N and I' (Father, Mother, N . . . and I?) saw the play on 18 March 1897. In the cast were Mr C. Aubrey Smith, Mr Bertram Wallis, Mr H.B. Irving, Mr George Alexander himself, Mr H.V. Esmond, Miss Julia Neilson and Miss Ellis Jeffreys. The incidental music to the play was specially composed by Mr Edward German, and an interval of music included works by Gounod and Wagner. The wigs were by W. Clarkson. There were 24 advertisements fitted on to the 7 × 10-inch back page, their wares including Singer sewing machines, Bryant & May matches, Younger's ales and Rose's lime juice – all familiar names a century later.

Mr and Mrs Kendal. Actor-manager William Kendal married Madge Robertson* in 1874 and they formed their own company. After some time at the old Prince of Wales with Squire and Marie Bancroft*, they moved, in 1879, to the St James's in partnership with John Hare (p. 86), and a period of prosperity came to the theatre. Four years later, by engaging young actor George Alexander, they ensured its greatest success, for he stayed and took over the management when they retired.

* These two actresses, plus sisters Ellen and Kate Terry, were, in the early 1860s, all youthful members of the same company in Bristol.

George Alexander (1858–1918). After a year managing the Avenue (p. 46), Alexander was at the St James's from 1891 until his death. He made it the high society theatre of London, presenting plays with settings and subjects appropriate to such audiences, by writers such as Wilde and Pinero – *Lady Windermere's Fan, The Second Mrs Tanqueray, His House in Order*, and so on. He was the first 'John Worthing' when *The Importance of Being Earnest* opened in 1895 (only to be taken off rather suddenly when Oscar Wilde went on trial), but the play was a great success when revived 15 years later. Alexander's good looks brought him matinée idol parts in plays like *If I Were King* (right, above) about poet François Villon and the French peasants' rebellion in the fifteenth century, and *Old Heidelberg* (right, below) which inspired Sigmund Romberg's 1924 musical play *The Student Prince*.

George Alexander with Marion Terry, 1892. Ellen Terry's younger sister Marion (1852–1930) was chosen by Alexander to create the part of 'Mrs Erlynne' in Oscar Wilde's *Lady Windermere's Fan*. She retired in 1923.

Electioneering, 1907. Alexander was an excellent businessman and committee-man, working for a number of theatrical and benevolent groups. He stood successfully as a Municipal Reform candidate for election to the London County Council, representing South St Pancras. Here he is (right) canvassing a bootmaker in Whitfield Street off Tottenham Court Road, accompanied by another Municipal Reform candidate, Mr Goldsmith (left).

Henry Ainley (1879–1945). Aged 23, he was chosen by Alexander to take the lead in a production of *Paulo and Francesca* at the St James's. His good looks and attractive voice ensured that thereafter he played in romances and in Shakespeare. In later life he undertook the role of 'Fedya' (left) in Mr and Mrs Aylmer Maude's translation of Tolstoy's *Zhivoi Trup (The Living Corpse)*.

St James's: *The Living Corpse*. Theatrical dictionaries tell us that the play, sometimes known as *Redemption*, was 'an attack on the evils of contemporary (1912) Russian marriage laws'. It is no surprise to find that two other beloved barn-stormers, John Barrymore and Donald Wolfit, also tackled the part.

Victoria Palace. The Royal Standard music hall originally stood at or near this site, but had to be rebuilt after the development of Victoria railway station, and was finally demolished in 1911. It was replaced by the buildings we know today, the last work of theatre architect Frank Matcham (right). Seating more than 1,500, its biggest success between the two world wars was *Me and My Girl*, starring Lupino Lane (overleaf). Unfortunately my photograph does not show the gilded statue of ballerina Anna Pavlova which stood until the Second World War on the very top of the dome, nor does it give any sign of the sliding roof which helps ventilate the auditorium. Eye-witnesses tell me that, in the days of heavy smokers, it was a sight to see the thick clouds of smoke that rose through the hole when the roof was opened in the interval.

Master 'Nipper' Lane. Member of a large stage family descended from a Lupino who married a Lane, Henry George Lupino (1892–1959), nicknamed 'Nipper', was acting by the age of four and became a favourite in pantomime. As Lupino Lane, he played comic roles here and in the United States in musical comedies and films. His Cockney character 'Bill Snibson' was included in the 1937 Victoria Palace hit *Me and My Girl*, where his talents (including juggling a bowler hat) helped the show to well over 1,000 performances, only terminated by the outbreak of war in 1939. It was very successfully revived five years later, and again at the Adelphi in 1985.

Ronald Shiner. He appeared in *Seagulls over Sorrento* which ran for more than three years at the Apollo, and specialized in 'wide boy' roles – ever on the look-out for a quick and slightly crooked deal, or a way to dodge an unpleasant duty. In 1945 he shone in R.F. Delderfield's *Worm's Eye View*, a farce about Royal Air Force recruits, which ran for some 500 performances at the Whitehall. It more than trebled that total on its return visit in 1947, followed by *Reluctant Heroes*, starring Ronnie again with Brian Rix, and the pattern was set for the next 22 years, when the 'Whitehall farces' held sway.

The Royal Court, Sloane Square. The first
theatre of this name, formerly a chapel,
stood 1870–87 on the south (Lower Sloane
Street) side of the square. While John Hare
was manager (1875–9), Ellen Terry played
very successfully in the comedy *New Men
and Old Acres* (in spite of critic George
Bernard Shaw's scathing comments on the
play). Also in the cast as 'Samuel Brown'
(the programme has been dated 27 January
1877 by its purchaser) was Mr Charles
Kelly, who was soon to become Ellen's
second husband. Seat prices were quoted
as Orchestra Stalls, 10s 0d/Dress Circle,
5s 0d/Boxes (bonnets allowed),
4s 0d/Amphitheatre, 2s 6d/Pit,
2s 0d/Gallery 1s 0d/Private Boxes, one
guinea to three guineas.

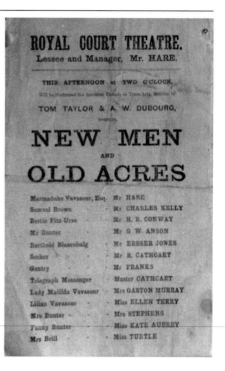

Arthur Wing Pinero (1855–1934).
Treading the boards is good preparation
for playwriting, and Pinero had ten
years on the stage before his *£200 a
Year* was presented at the Globe in
1877. After some success at the St
James's, by 1885 he was producing
farces for both old and new Royal
Courts (the latter rising on its present
site in 1888). They included *The
Magistrate, The School Mistress* and
Dandy Dick. For *The Second Mrs
Tanqueray* Mrs Patrick Campbell was
engaged for the name part; *Trelawney
of the 'Wells'* was first produced at the
Sloane Square theatre and has since
been revived and turned into a musical.
Controversy reigned when the
management of Vedrenne and Granville-
Barker (p. 40) put on eleven Shaw
plays; in 1956 John Osborne's *Look
Back in Anger* heralded the arrival of
the 'Angry Young Man'.

The Royal Victoria (Old Vic), The Cut, Lambeth. The theatre now revered as part of our Shakespearean tradition did not always aim so high. The original building on the site (left), opened on 11 May 1818 and was named the Royal Coburg to honour its patrons Princess Charlotte and her husband Prince Leopold of Saxe-Coburg. It served up popular sensational melodramas. Materials from the nearby Savoy Palace, recently demolished, were recycled and an outstanding feature of the theatre was its 63-mirrored curtain reflecting the whole auditorium, but so heavy that it had to be dismantled before it could pull the roof down. (The modern curtain, studded with small mirrors, echoes the idea.) After refurbishment and renaming in honour of the princess who became Queen Victoria four years later (married to another Prince of Saxe-Coburg), its reputation deteriorated.

Transformation of the Old Vic by Emma Cons. Musician Lilian Baylis was summoned home from South Africa by her aunt Miss Cons in 1895 to help run the temperance hall she had established at the Old Vic. Seventeen years later Miss Baylis inherited the theatre and embarked on setting a record for the first company to present every Shakespeare play. Miss Baylis (front) is here with Dorothy Green and John Gielgud, who made his debut at the Old Vic, aged 17, as the herald in *Henry V*.

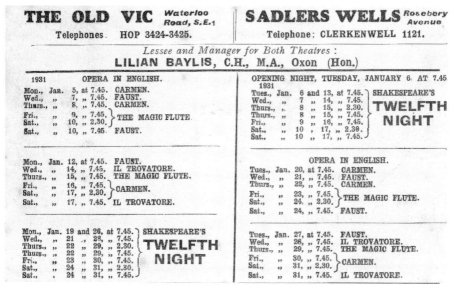

Old Vic/Sadler's Wells, 1931. Miss Baylis acquired Sadlers Wells (p. 128) for her opera and ballet companies which from the opening in 1931 until 1935 alternated with the drama company. She wrote on 10 January 1931 on the reverse of this postcard: 'We had a good opening – now it remains to get people infected with "the Wells habit"'.

JULIET.   ROMEO.

MARGARET HALSTAN.   HARCOURT WILLIAMS.

Harcourt Williams (1880–1957), Old Vic director 1929–34. He began acting at 18 and in a distinguished career performed with Benson, Ellen Terry, Alexander, Irving and John Barrymore. His time at the Old Vic began with disapproval and ended with acclaim; his introduction into Shakespeare of the realism and simplicity eschewed by Granville-Barker was only gradually accepted by audiences. He was with the Old Vic company again in 1946 in New York. The photograph shows a young Williams on tour in 1905 with Margaret Helston in *Romeo and Juliet*. He was renowned for his discerning delivery and high regard for Shakespeare's words.

Edith Evans (1888–1976). Her first role was as Shakespeare's Cressida with William Poel's Elizabethan Stage Society in 1912. She was at the Old Vic in 1925–6, again in 1936 and in 1958, ending director Michael Benthall's 'Five-Year Plan' to emulate Miss Baylis in staging all Shakespeare's plays, when she played Queen Katherine in *Henry VIII*. She also excelled in Restoration roles, and in some Shaw plays. She was created Dame Commander of the British Empire in 1946.

Eric Portman (1903–69). After touring with Robert Courtneidge's company (p. 147), Eric Portman joined the Old Vic in 1927 and, the following year, played Romeo to Jean Forbes-Robertson's Juliet (p. 34). Later he appeared in modern plays, including several of Terence Rattigan's. In 1950 he starred in the long-running *His Excellency* by Dorothy and Campbell Christie at the Prince's (later Shaftesbury). He also starred in a number of movies notably in the Second World War (*One of Our Aircraft is Missing*, 1941, and *A Canterbury Tale*, 1944). He last appeared on stage in a revival of Galsworthy's *Justice* the year before his death.

A Midsummer Night's Dream, Old Vic, 1938. Tyrone Guthrie's production used Mendelssohn's incidental music and Oliver Messel's decor. By borrowing Robert Helpmann from the Sadler's Wells ballet company and matching his Oberon with the delicate Titania of Vivien Leigh (p. 112) a play resulted where the fairies outshone the mortals, if *Theatre World*'s critic is to be believed; this in spite of a splendid interpretation of Bottom by Ralph Richardson (arm raised). Richardson (1902–83) was knighted in 1947, and is remembered on the first night of each new play at the National Theatre by the firing of 'Ralph's Rocket' from the roof, a tradition that he began.

Denis Quilley (b. 1927). A drama school and company for younger players, led by George Devine, began late in 1946 and came to be called the Young Vic; it lasted till 1951. The idea was revived almost 20 years later. Denis Quilley acted with this company and with the Old Vic, and is seen here as 'Dick Shelton' in the Young Vic production of *The Black Arrow*, adapted from R.L. Stevenson.

Section Three

HAYMARKET & PICCADILLY CIRCUS

Theatre Royal, Haymarket. Although a theatre known as the Little Theatre in the Hay opened here in 1720, with playwright Henry Fielding of Tom Jones *fame as manager in 1735, it had to wait over 40 years to join those other venerable establishments in Drury Lane and Covent Garden, in having a royal patent. John Nash designed the new building that went up in 1821; the six exterior columns we see today were his. In 1837 gas-lighting was belatedly installed to replace the candlelight. For 25 years (1853–78) comedy actor-manager John B. Buckstone ran the theatre . . . and now is said to haunt it.*

Squire and Lady Bancroft. Squire Bancroft (left) met Marie Wilton when both were playing in the provinces, and they married in 1867. After a few years at the Prince of Wales (p. 82) they moved to the Haymarket, where they continued their self-appointed task of raising theatrical standards and improving the actors' lot, especially regarding salaries. Mrs Bancroft's name on an advertisement (below), along with other leading actresses, was adequate endorsement of the product. Squire Bancroft was knighted in 1897; at 85, upright and elegant as ever, he accompanied Lilian Baylis (p. 63) and other stage luminaries standing on the site of the new Sadler's Wells theatre (p. 128).

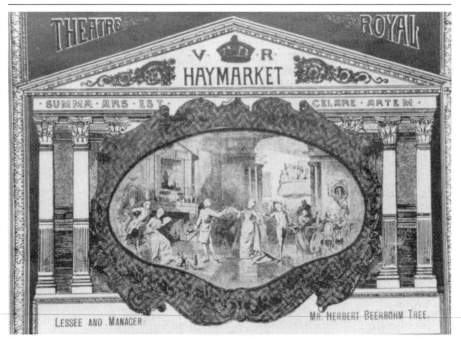

First production of *Trilby*, Theatre Royal, 1896. The cast included Herbert Beerbohm Tree as 'Svengali' the evil hypnotist, Dorothea Baird as 'Trilby O'Ferrall' his victim, Lionel Brough and H.V. Esmond. George du Maurier had dramatized his own novel, and his son Gerald made one of his first stage appearances as 'Dodor'. The programme (gold and crimson cover, above) also advertised 'The Trilby Souvenir, on sale price two shillings', an ornamental folder with portraits of the seven principals.

Winifred Emery (1862–1924). The fourth generation of the Emery family to tread the boards, she was acting by the age of eight and was appearing in London at twelve. Five years later she made her mature debut and subsequently toured the United States in Irving's company. She married actor-manager Cyril Maude (p. 48) in 1888 and became leading lady of the Theatre Royal Haymarket when he took over there, in partnership with Frederick Harrison, eight years later.

The Clandestine Marriage. Written in 1766 by David Garrick (p. 87) and Colman the Elder (once owner of the Little Theatre in the Hay), the play was presented at the Haymarket in 1903 under Maude's management. The writer of the postcard from which the scene is taken states that Mr Allan Aynesworth as 'Canton' is on the left, and right is Mr Lionel Rignold as 'Sterling'.

Cousin Kate, a comedy by Hubert Henry Davies. It was was staged by Maude in 1903 with Ellis Jeffreys (left) in the title role and Beatrice Ferrar (right) as 'Amy'.

Beauty and the Barge, c. 1904. Left to right, Frederick Volpe, Jessie Bateman, Rita Jolivit, Mrs Calvert, Robert Bottomley, Cyril Maude and Edmund Maurice appear in a scene from this play by L.N. Parker and W.W. Jacobs. Maude's playing of 'Captain Barley' was considered a masterpiece of make-up and interpretation. On the same bill, at the Theatre Royal, was a curtain-raiser which also featured Maude himself, *The Monkey's Paw* by W.W. Jacobs. Strange to say, while *Beauty and the Barge* seems to have sunk without trace, the short, horrific *The Monkey's Paw* has survived to be performed occasionally to this day, and the story read on radio.

John Barrymore (1882–1942). Younger brother of Lionel and Ethel Barrymore (p. 105), John was one of the American matinée idols of the pre-First World War stage. Hitherto known for his light comedy roles, in 1922 he amazed New York audiences with his brilliant interpretation of Shakespeare's *Hamlet*, repeated at the Theatre Royal, Haymarket, three years later. The story goes that he never fully accepted the West End tradition of interval refreshments taken in the auditorium and, on one occasion when the play had resumed, paused in mid-soliloquy and came to the footlights to protest about the still-imbibing audience and its 'tea . . . tea . . . tea'.

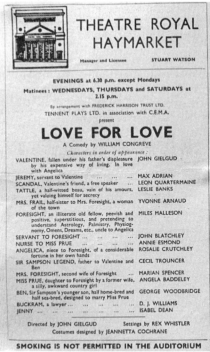

THEATRE ROYAL HAYMARKET

Manager and Licensee   STUART WATSON

EVENINGS at 6.30 p.m. except Mondays
Matinees : WEDNESDAYS, THURSDAYS and SATURDAYS at 2.15 p.m.

By arrangement with FREDERICK HARRISON TRUST LTD.
TENNENT PLAYS LTD. in association with C.E.M.A.
present

LOVE FOR LOVE

A Comedy by WILLIAM CONGREVE

Characters in order of appearance :

VALENTINE, fallen under his father's displeasure by his expensive way of living. In love with Angelica	JOHN GIELGUD
JEREMY, servant to Valentine	MAX ADRIAN
SCANDAL, Valentine's friend, a free speaker	LEON QUARTERMAINE
TATTLE, a half-witted beau, vain of his amours, yet valuing himself for secrecy	LESLIE BANKS
MRS. FRAIL, half-sister to Mrs. Foresight, a woman of the town	YVONNE ARNAUD
FORESIGHT, an illiterate old fellow, peevish and positive, superstitious, and pretending to understand Astrology, Palmistry, Physiognomy, Omens, Dreams, etc., uncle to Angelica	MILES MALLESON
SERVANT TO FORESIGHT	JOHN BLATCHLEY
NURSE TO MISS PRUE	ANNIE ESMOND
ANGELICA, niece to Foresight, of a considerable fortune in her own hands	ROSALIE CRUTCHLEY
SIR SAMPSON LEGEND, father to Valentine and Ben	CECIL TROUNCER
MRS. FORESIGHT, second wife of Foresight	MARIAN SPENCER
MISS PRUE, daughter to Foresight by a former wife, a silly, awkward country girl	ANGELA BADDELEY
BEN, Sir Sampson's younger son, half home-bred and half sea-bred, designed to marry Miss Prue	GEORGE WOODBRIDGE
BUCKRAM, a lawyer	D. J. WILLIAMS
JENNY	ISABEL DEAN

Directed by JOHN GIELGUD   Settings by REX WHISTLER
Costumes designed by JEANNETTA COCHRANE

SMOKING IS NOT PERMITTED IN THE AUDITORIUM

— SYNOPSIS OF SCENES —

The Scene in London—1695

ACT I. Scene 1. Valentine's Lodgings. Morning
Singer : ERIC GOLDIE
Scene 2. Foresight's House. The same day
Scene 3. The same. The same evening

INTERVAL

ACT II. Scene 1. Valentine's Lodgings. The next morning
Singer : ERIC GOLDIE
Scene 2. Foresight's House. Later in the day

The incidental music arranged and the songs "A Nymph and a Swain," "Cynthia" and "Charmion," composed to Congreve's own words by LESLIE BRIDGEWATER.
Music on sale in the Theatre)

Dance arranged by Andree Howard   The play lit by Hamish Wilson
Costumes by B. J. Simmons & Co., Ltd., 7 and 8 King Street, Covent Garden, W.C.2
Wigs by Nathanwigs, 12 Panton Street, S.W.1   Shoes by H. & M. Rayne, Ltd.
Stockings by Kayser-Bondor

Scenery painted by Alick Johnstone
Built by Brunskill & Loveday
The play furnished by the Old Times Furnishing Company
Properties by Robinson Bros. (Jewellers) Ltd.
Electrical equipment by the Strand Electric & Engineering Co., Ltd.

Box Office (M. FLYNN) open daily from 10 a.m. to 6.30 p.m.   Phone : WHI 9832

NOTICE

In the event of an Air Raid Warning an announcement will be made by means of an illuminated box sign installed immediately in front of the footlights. Patrons are advised to remain in the Theatre, but those wishing to leave will be directed to the nearest official shelter, after which the performance will be continued for so long as is practicable.

GENERAL MANAGER	For	ELSIE BEYER
Stage Managers	TENNENT PLAYS LTD.	ROBIN ANDERSON and MARY LYNN
Press Representative		RICHARD CLOWES

Stage Director - (for Haymarket Theatre) - CHARLES LA TROBE

SMOKING IS NOT PERMITTED IN THE AUDITORIUM

War-time programme: Congreve's *Love for Love*. CEMA, co-presenters of the play, was the Council for the Encouragement of Music and the Arts, set up in 1940 to administer grants to keep music and drama flourishing in the war years. Do read the NOTICE on the right-hand page concerning air-raids; on another page is a polite reminder that 'the booking hall, Piccadilly Circus station, is NOT an air-raid shelter'.

Italian Opera House, *c*. 1880. A place of entertainment has stood on this site for almost three centuries, beginning with Sir John Vanbrugh and William Congreve's theatre, the Queen's, where Handel first conducted his opera *Rinaldo*. After a disastrous fire in 1789 a new theatre, the King's, after the reigning monarch, continued the tradition of dance and song. In the 1840s the 'Swedish Nightingale' Jenny Lind sang there several times.

Herbert Beerbohm Tree (1853–1917). Tree took a mere nine years from his professional debut to his first theatre management, of the Comedy. Only months later he was in the Haymarket at the Theatre Royal, where his huge successes over the next ten years put him in a financial position to re-build the Italian Opera House in 1897, naming it Her Majesty's. There he remained (here as Hamlet in 1905) until his death, earning a reputation for extravagant and colourful presentations of Shakespeare and other classic plays, together with adaptations of tales by Charles Dickens and William Makepeace Thackeray.

Her Majesty's. Though the postcard view on the left is dated about 1900, very little of its outward appearance has changed since. Tree called it 'my beautiful theatre' and Charles Phipps's design, which incorporated the neighbouring Carlton Hotel in 1897, is most surely very pleasing to the eye. To the rear, connecting Pall Mall and Charles II Street, is the Royal Opera Arcade. Take a walk through it and try to imagine the scene in 1911 when it was used as the dressing-room for 300 actors taking part in the gala performance of *Julius Caesar* to celebrate the coronation of George V and Queen Mary. The Victorian cartoon (right) advertises the theatre as HER Majesty's, which has been its name again since 1952.

Herbert Beerbohm Tree as Malvolio, 1901. Shakespeare's *Twelfth Night*, written 1599–1600, provided Tree with a splendid opportunity to give an eccentric portrayal of the Lady Olivia's self-important steward Malvolio, who is 'taken down a peg or two' by the tricks of other members of the household. Tree founded a drama school which was housed in the dome of the theatre until it moved to its own headquarters in Gower Street, becoming the Royal Academy of Dramatic Art (RADA). Tree was knighted in 1909.

Constance Collier (1878–1955). She was a child actor and later joined the Gaiety Girls and other managements, before reaching Tree's company at Her Majesty's in 1901. She stayed there for the next seven years, playing a number of Shakespearean roles. She was also 'Nancy' to Tree's 'Fagin' in Comyns Carr's adaptation of Dickens's *Oliver Twist*. When John Barrymore (p. 72) came to London in 1925 and played Hamlet, across the road at the Theatre Royal, she was Queen Gertrude.

Mrs Patrick Campbell (1865–1940, left) and Isadora Duncan (1878–1927). Tree's last success was in 1914 as 'Professor Higgins' in the first London production of *Pygmalion* which George Bernard Shaw wrote for Mrs Campbell (when she was almost 50 years old), to play the Cockney flower-seller 'Eliza Doolittle'. She had already created the Pinero roles of 'Paula' in the controversial *The Second Mrs Tanqueray* (1893) and of the eponymous *Notorious Mrs Ebbsmith* two years later, and played in Shakespeare and Ibsen. She introduced the young Isadora Duncan (far right, with her American pupil and assistant 'Irma') into London society in 1900. Though Isadora danced for Tree and his wife, and at the home of Mrs Wyndham (Mary Moore, p. 79), and was for a short time in Benson's company for *A Midsummer Night's Dream*, her barefoot interpretive dancing failed to appeal to the English audiences of that time, and she and her entourage moved on to Europe.

The School for Scandal at His Majesty's. Left to right: Edward Terry, Ellis Jeffreys, H.V. Esmond, Suzanne Sheldon, Marie Lohr, Herbert Beerbohm Tree. This all-star cast was assembled for Tree's revival of R.B. Sheridan's 1777 play; Basil Gill, Lionel Brough (p. 16) and Godfrey Tearle (p. 13) were also involved.

The Comedy, Panton Street. With the Prince and Princess of Wales at the opening night in 1881, and early successes with Audan's opera *La Mascotte*, and Lewis Waller in *Monsieur Beaucaire* (left, above), the Comedy has had a relatively happy career. From 1956 to 1968 it was used for the staging of banned or controversial plays by the New Watergate Theatre Club, until censorship was abolished.

E.W. Hornung's *Raffles*, 1906. Gerald du Maurier (left) brought 'the gentleman cracksmith' to the stage of the Comedy in a highly successful adaptation of Hornung's thriller. Laurence Irving (right), thus presented a good example of the theatre's own 'generation game': Gerald was the son of artist and novelist George du Maurier (p. 69) and Laurence the younger son of Henry Irving. Laurence and his actress wife Mabel Hackney died when the *Empress of Ireland*, in which they were sailing from Quebec for Liverpool, sank in the St Lawrence estuary. Herbert Beerbohm Tree, with whom he had recently appeared in *Othello*, wrote his obituary.

Mrs Dot, 1908. A number of W. Somerset Maugham plays were produced in the Edwardian heyday of the drawing-room comedy, including *Lady Frederick*, *Jack Straw*, and *The Explorer*. These three, together with *Mrs Dot*, which starred Marie Tempest (here with her third husband Graham Browne), set a record for Maugham when they were being produced simultaneously in West End theatres.

Piccadilly Circus, London.

The Criterion, Piccadilly Circus. This delightful subterranean 600-seater (sharing with the Criterion restaurant the glass canopy to the right of the statue of Eros in the postcard view above) was designed in 1874 by Thomas Verity with a wealth of interior detail.

Mary Moore, Criterion actor-manager 1919–31. The street-level box office area is decorated with classical scenes on ceiling panels and tiled walls, and a large portrait of Mary Moore. She inherited the theatre from her second husband Charles Wyndham (p. 104). One descends to the auditorium by a staircase where more tiled walls bear the names of great composers, and, among the gilded ornaments within, Wyndham's monogram can be seen.

Sixty years at the Criterion. *Fourteen Days* (*c.* 1885) with a girl smoking a cigarette, *The Mollusc* (1907), *A Little Bit of Fluff* (1915) showing a girl's bare leg, and *Ambrose Applejohn's Adventure* (1921) were some of the successes at the Criterion. The 1922 play *The Dippers* was notable for a different reason. Edith and Percy Thompson were returning home from the 'Cri' after seeing it, when Edith's young lover Fred Bywaters waylaid and murdered her husband. It led to a notorious trial at the Old Bailey. Kay Hammond as 'Diana' (above, left) and Lueen McGrath as 'Jacqueline' appeared in Terence Rattigan's *French Without Tears* (1936–9). The BBC used the underground auditorium as a wartime light entertainment studio. Looking north towards Shaftesbury Avenue in about 1921, Cyril Maude in *Grumpy* is advertised on the side of an open-topped bus (below, left) and Nelson 'Bunch' Keys (who had been in *The Arcadians* in 1909) was in Charles B. Cochran's revue *London Paris and New York*, at the London Pavilion.

The London Pavilion, Piccadilly Circus. The old-style music-hall interior that opened in 1885 was soon converted to the normal rows of seats throughout the auditorium, where many famous entertainers could be seen.

Albert Chevalier. He started out as a straight actor, made a hit at the Pavilion with his first attempt at Cockney patter and songs like 'My Old Dutch' and 'Knocked 'em in the Old Kent Road'. Harry Tate (p. 152) and Charles Coborn were other 'turns' engaged. In 1934 the building was converted into a cinema, keeping the same name.

The Prince of Wales. An eighteenth-century theatre known, by 1865, as 'the Dust Hole' because of the depths to which it had sunk, it was rescued by actress Marie Wilton (Mrs Bancroft, p. 68) and, with royal approval, named after the future Edward VII, who attended the reopening. Twenty years later it was once more derelict and was replaced in 1905 by the Scala (p. 153).

The Prince's, built to a C.J. Phipps' design on the corner of Coventry Street and Oxenden Street in 1884, and given the full title two years later, saw performances by Hawtrey, Tree, Langtry, Campbell, Forbes-Robertson and Tempest before the end of the nineteenth century. Musical comedies of George Edwardes, shows presented by André Charlot and non-stop revues followed. The theatre was demolished and rebuilt in 1937.

The School Girl, 1902. While carving a niche for himself as a light comedian with overtones of a 'toff' or a 'silly ass', G.P. Huntley appeared in this musical comedy at the Prince of Wales. Starting on their stage careers in the same play were Pauline Chase (p. 101) and Billie Burke (p. 96). *Three Little Maids*, starring Marie Studholme (above) and Edna May (p. 42), *Lady Madcap* and *Miss Hook of Holland* followed, all presented by Frank Curzon. The last-mentioned of these had words and music by Paul Rubens, who also wrote the ever-popular ballad, 'I Love the Moon'. This postcard portrait of Marie Studholme advertised her appearance in *Miss Hook of Holland* at the King's Theatre, Hammersmith.

Moonbeams concert party. A light comedian making an early West End appearance in *Charlot's Revue of 1924* at the Prince of Wales was Leonard Henry (far right). He later became one of the BBC's radio stars. Thorpe Bates (far left) was an established performer and fine singer, for whom Ivor Novello wrote 'Dear Eyes that Shine'. He appeared in *The Rebel Maid* at the Empire, Leicester Square (p. 126), singing 'The Fishermen of England', and was 'Beppo' in *The Maid of the Mountains* at Daly's in 1917.

The Prince of Wales rises again, 1937. This drawing of 'the new Prince of Wales theatre, Piccadilly Circus, W.1 (foundation stone laid by Miss Gracie Fields)' appeared in a stage magazine a month after the reopening. *Les Folies de Paris et Londres* was on offer 'non-stop 2–11.30', starring American entertainer Eddie Foy with 'fifty glorious glamour girls'. Seats cost from 2s 6d including tax. During and after the Second World War impresario George Black raised morale with his successful shows which brought us, if only for a few years, that unique and unforgettable personality Sid Field.

Section Four

CHARING CROSS ROAD
& LEICESTER SQUARE

David Garrick and William Shakespeare, 1769. The Garrick is one of the few West End

theatres bearing the name of an actor, although it was built more than a century after

Garrick's death. This commemorative sketch recalls the Shakespeare jubilee pageant

arranged by Garrick at Stratford-on-Avon in 1769. Though Richard III, Lear and

Macbeth were among his most successful roles he did not include anything by the Bard but

used instead his own material.

The Garrick, Charing Cross Road. The theatre was built for John Hare (left) in 1889 with W.S. Gilbert's money (proceeds from some of the Savoy operas), to the design of Emden and Phipps. It was the second London theatre of that name, the first being in Leman Street, Whitechapel, from 1831–46 and (after a fire) from 1854–81. Tree (pp. 73–7) appeared there in 1879, very early in his career. While excavating the subterranean auditorium, workmen came across an ancient stream, known of in Roman times. The Northern Line of the London underground rail system now runs below the theatre: occasional rumblings may be disconcerting in moments of dramatic suspense, but can sometimes augment war-like sound effects. *The Plough and the Stars* benefited in this way very recently (1995).

David Garrick (1717–79). Born in Hereford, Garrick was educated in Lichfield where he met Dr Samuel Johnson, with whom he travelled to London at the age of 20. His first stage appearances were in Ipswich and London four years later, and he was quickly engaged for Drury Lane. His distinguished acting-managing career spanned 35 years during which he was responsible for a number of theatrical reforms and innovations including a more natural, less declamatory delivery of lines. He also wrote or adapted 40 plays and collaborated with George Colman the Elder in *The Clandestine Marriage* (p. 70) in 1766. Garrick had put on Colman's first play at Drury Lane six years earlier.

Garrick's villa at Hampton Court. Garrick was unkindly described as lacking the height for heroic roles, as vain and quick-tempered, quarrelsome and snobbish. Yet we are told that the grounds of his magnificent mansion by the Thames were the setting for a number of al fresco rehearsals for younger performers. He would walk for hours with them in the gardens, generously imparting the secrets of his success. He retired here with his wife Eva Maria Violetti in 1776 and died three years later, being buried in Westminster Abbey. His memorial stone is next to that of his old friend Johnson.

Garrick's London home. From 1772 until his death in 1779, Garrick's London home was at 5 Adelphi Terrace, Strand. The blue plaque commemorated the distinction bestowed on the premises, occupied by his widow for many years; she lived to be 98.

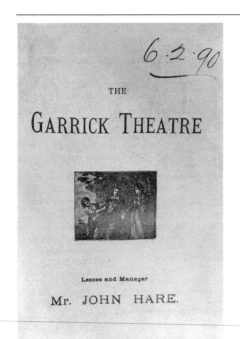

6·2·90

THE

GARRICK THEATRE

Lessee and Manager

Mr. JOHN HARE.

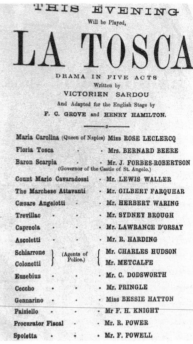

Programme for play *La Tosca*, 1900. John Hare (1844–1921) produced plays with such luminaries as Johnston Forbes-Robertson, Lewis Waller and Mrs Patrick Campbell. His stage career began at the age of 21 at the Bancrofts' Prince of Wales, and he was in management at the Royal Court (p. 61) and the St James's (p. 54) before opening the Garrick. He continued to act in favourite roles like 'Goldfinch' in *A Pair of Spectacles*, 'Old Eccles' in *Caste*, and the eponymous 'Gay Lord Quex', and was knighted four years before his death.

Arthur Bourchier (1863–1927) (left) and his first wife Violet Vanbrugh leased the Garrick for six years from 1900 and gave it back some of the prestige it had lost following Hare's departure in 1895, with a range of plays including Shakespeare, Pinero and J.M. Barrie. Violet Vanbrugh (1867–1942) had early acting experience at Toole's (p. 9) and the Lyceum (p. 19) with Irving. Her younger sister Irene excelled as Pinero heroines and also in Barrie plays. The Bourchiers had an apartment 'over the shop' reached by a staircase from the Garrick stage. The friendly ghost of Arthur Bourchier (a founder-member in 1885 of OUDS, the Oxford University Dramatic Society) is sometimes sensed, having descended the stair to encourage some nervous player with a pat on the shoulder.

The Fairy's Dilemma. Violet Vanbrugh starred in this play, which was advertised on horse-drawn omnibuses, seen here in Piccadilly Circus, as well as outside the theatre (below). Violet and Irene Vanbrugh's brother, Sir Kenneth Barnes (1878–1957), was principal of the Royal Academy of Dramatic Art (p. 75) for more than 45 years. The Academy's own theatre is called the Vanbrugh.

Henry VIII. The Bourchiers appeared together for Tree in 1910–11 as King Henry and Queen Katherine to his Cardinal Wolsey, in Shakespeare's last play.

Oscar Asche (1871–1936) and Lily Brayton (1876–1953). This was the second husband and wife team to run the Garrick. Asche, an Australian, had next to no dramatic training but at the age of 22 found his way into Benson's company where, over the next eight years, his size and athleticism ensured steady promotion up the cast list. With Lily he moved to the Adelphi where their partnership in *The Taming of the Shrew* made them stars; it was calculated they played it over 1,500 times, in London and on tour. A successful *As You Like It* at His Majesty's was followed by *Kismet* at the Garrick.

Poster for *Kismet*, 1911. The play opened on 19 April and received a visit from George V within a month. Asche was 'Hajj the beggar' and his wife played 'Marsinah'. The play was highly successful and created a fashion for slave bangles and other Eastern jewellery. It was written by American Edward Knoblock, whose other work included *Milestones* (p. 142) with Arnold Bennett. Another version of *Kismet*, based on the music of Borodin, was seen at the Stoll, Kingsway, in the mid-1950s. Asche presented the long-running oriental musical *Chu Chin Chow* (p. 77) at His Majesty's; theatregoers sitting in the perfumed auditorium for the last performance in 1921 had paid double-price for their seats. It was almost the end of an era.

Sam Livesey. Here we find another theatrical dynasty, for Sam was carried on stage at the age of six months. He first played in London in 1912 at the Royal Court, and took *Kismet* round the country with the Garrick touring company. His three sons were all actors, though none could equal his record for a first appearance. They were: Jack (debut aged 15), Barrie (at 17) and Roger (at 11), whose leading role in *The Life and Death of Colonel Blimp* helped make that morale-booster one of the film hits of war-weary 1943.

Garrick publicity postcards. For a few years after the First World War Charles B. Cochran, already at the London Pavilion (pp. 80–1), leased the Garrick. It was 'by arrangement' with him that Percy Hutchinson (left, playing 'Lieutenant Clive Stanton') and Alfred Butt presented *The Luck of the Navy* by Clifford Mills. 'See the sensational submarine scene, as played before HM the Queen', says the blurb.

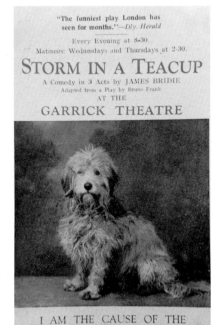

"The funniest play London has seen for months."—*Dly. Herald*

Every Evening at 8·30.
Matinees: Wednesdays and Thursdays at 2·30.

STORM IN A TEACUP
A Comedy in 3 Acts by JAMES BRIDIE
Adapted from a Play by Bruno Frank
AT THE

GARRICK THEATRE

I AM THE CAUSE OF THE "STORM."

James Bridie's *Storm in a Teacup* came to the Garrick in 1936; it was an adaptation from the German of Bruno Frank's *Sturm in Wasserglass*, given a Scottish setting.

The Coliseum, St Martin's Lane, 1906.
Thousands flocked to see the marvels of
the new theatre (London's largest), built to
the design of Frank Matcham. It was the
concept of Oswald Stoll, the Australian-
Irish showman whose career began at the
age of 14, when he was left to run his
family's Liverpool music hall. Four variety
shows a day were staged from the
Coliseum's opening on Christmas Eve
1904; Stoll aimed to eradicate the
vulgarities committed by previous
comedians and to promote family shows.
The glittering sphere (above) has 'revolved'
from the first, though nowadays
intermittent lighting creates the effect on a
stationary globe. Four figures at the base of
the square tower represent Art, Music,
Science and Literature. The theatre claimed
to be the first in Europe with passenger
lifts to all floors. A roof garden survived
into the 1950s, and the elegant tea-room
(below) attracted many.

THE LONDON COLISEUM.

ONE OF THE
TEA ROOMS

THE LONDON COLISEUM AUDITORIUM.

Traditionally the royal box at the Coliseum (see centre above, and p. 6) is sited to the best advantage, but the 2,358 seats (plus 150 standing) in amphitheatre style are all well situated for the appreciation of large-scale works. Stoll's uplifting policy was not wholly popular, so, in 1906, he presented *The Revue* with a cast of 300, starring Billie Burke (1884–1970) (left), whose real first name was Ethelbert. Stoll's change of direction misfired and for more than a year the theatre was dark. Lowering his sights, in late 1907 he reopened as a music hall, and for the next 20 years performers like Harry Lauder, Vesta Tilley, Harry Tate (p. 152) and Albert Chevalier (p. 81), plus ballet and interpolated scenes from Shakespeare and other classics ensured packed houses. In 1924 comedian Nellie Wallace set a record by appearing in every one of the 635 performances of *The Whirl of the World* – and then took it on tour. A television demonstration took place on the stage in 1930.

EMILE LITTLER

ST. MARTIN'S LANE, LONDON, W.C.2

Telephones: TEMPLE BAR 6160 9873-9874

Please attend audition at _Coliseum Theatre W·C·2_

on _Tuesday April 15_ **at** _10·30_ **a.m.**

Dancers please come prepared to dance.

Ballet dancers please bring block shoes.

Singers please bring song.

Ballet Essential

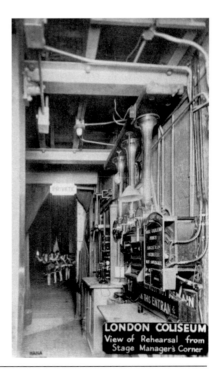

LONDON COLISEUM
View of Rehearsal from
Stage Manager's Corner

Auditions and rehearsals at the Coliseum. Hopeful actors, singers and dancers get to hear of auditions through advertisements in *The Stage* and other theatrical papers, or from their agent. The agonies and frustrations of this particular kind of competition were fully explored in Marvin Hamisch's musical *A Chorus Line*, seen at the Theatre Royal, Drury Lane, in 1976 and since made into a movie. The notification (above) was sent to a young dancer at an address in Devon. The view of the stage from the stage manager's corner (below) is a good example of the contrast between the glamour seen by the audience and the backstage technicalities necessary to present that image.

LONDON COLISEUM
Below the Revolving Stage

Stage-effects at the Coliseum. The revolving stage (above) was the first in Britain, developed from a German idea eight years earlier. One of its chief uses is to enable a succession of new sets to be prepared and then revealed, but Stoll employed it in his first show to represent the running of the Epsom Derby with real horses. A similar spectacle had been tried in 1909 at Drury Lane in *The Whip*, but nothing could be done to guarantee the right horse won every time. *White Horse Inn* at the Coliseum in 1931 was the first of many spectacular musical comedies. In it was boy actor Jimmy Hanley (left). He became better known in movies; his first was *Little Friend* with Nova Pilbeam (p. 153) in 1934, and he gave a memorable portrayal of 'Cobb' in *Gaslight* (called *Angel Street* in the United States) six years later.

Musicals, Cinerama, opera and ballet at the Coliseum. A succession of home-grown and American musicals filled the theatre, but in 1961 the giant film company MGM took a seven-year lease for Cinerama. Still London's largest theatre, the Coliseum is well suited to its present use (since 1968) as the home of English National Opera. Visiting ballet companies like the Bolshoi and the Kirov have also used the venue in recent years.

Violet Melnotte (1852–1935) of the Duke of York's. 'Madame' began her London career with Wyndham's company and went into management at the Avenue (p. 46) at the age of 33. In 1892 she had the Trafalgar Square theatre built in a then dark, unfashionable, muddy street called St Martin's Lane. Only three years later, royal approval was obtained to change the name to commemorate the Duke who became George V. Although an attractive building (by Emden), it did not do too well so Madame, while retaining a fierce proprietorial interest in it, leased it to a succession of promoters. The ghost of a woman in black, occasionally seen in the circle bar, is thought to be Madame.

Charles Frohman (1860–1915). In 1897 the American impresario took the first lease (for 19 years) of the Duke of York's. He had several theatres in the United States, and five in London. Many leading names of the Edwardian stage can be found on his play-bills: William Gillette, William Terriss, Evelyn Willard, Edna May, Joseph Coyne, H.B. Irving, Muriel Beaumont, Gerald du Maurier, Irene Vanbrugh – the last four in *The Admirable Crichton* (p. 102). He was a passenger on the *Lusitania*, travelling back to England from New York during the First World War, when an enemy U-boat torpedoed her in the Atlantic in May 1915.

The Adventure of Lady Ursula, 1898. The play by Anthony Hope was the first presented by Frohman at the Duke of York's, with Evelyn Millard looking most attractive in her eighteenth-century breeches role in brocade coat, lace-trimmed shirt and powdered wig. She is seen here with Herbert Waring, who had played the lead in an earlier successful costume drama *Under the Red Robe* at the Haymarket. In 1900 Evelyn Millard was appearing in David Belasco's one-act play *Madame Butterfly* when composer Giacomo Puccini saw it; his opera based on the story was written four years later.

Two 'Peter Pans'. Nina Boucicault was the first actress to play the title role in *Peter Pan*, at the Duke of York's in December 1904. It was a brilliant combined effort by Charles Frohman and his producer D.G. Boucicault (Nina's brother, known as 'Dot'), in putting on an adaptation of a story by J.M. Barrie, who had written *The Admirable Crichton*.

The presentation of *Peter Pan* became an annual Christmas tradition, and, in 1905, Cissie Loftus took the name part, understudied by Pauline Chase (left). Like a fairy tale within a fairy tale, Miss Loftus fell ill on tour, Miss Chase seized her chance and was rewarded by having the lead for the next eight years. Madge Titheradge was 'Peter' in 1914; it was ironic that she and Miss Boucicault should appear together at the Duke of York's in 1927 in one of Noël Coward's few disasters, *Home Chat*.

Peter Pan statue, Kensington Gardens. Barrie arranged for all proceeds of the play to go to the Great Ormond Street Hospital for Sick Children, known as Peter Pan's Hospital. The play has been produced every Christmas since 1904 except (according to my 1951 programme from the Scala theatre) for two years at the beginning of the Second World War, filling various London theatres and annually arousing interest in the choice of actress to play 'Peter'. They included Gladys Cooper (1923–4), Jean Forbes-Robertson (1927–34, 1938), Nova Pilbeam (1935) and Glynis Johns (1943). Henry Ainley, Gerald du Maurier, Ralph Richardson and Seymour Hicks likewise were all 'Captain Hooks'.

The Admirable Crichton, 1902. To set the scene, the Earl of Loam and his family and guests including 'the Hon. Ernest Woolley' (Gerald du Maurier, right) have been shipwrecked on a desert island. No one has any idea how to cope, and it is Crichton (H.B. Irving), until then the perfect butler, who takes control and eventually becomes king of the island. Compare this picture with *Raffles* (p. 78), which has another of Henry Irving's sons pointing at Gerald du Maurier. This Frohman-Barrie-Boucicault triumph ran for 328 performances at the Duke of York's.

Ellen Terry, 1905. Barrie wrote *Alice-sit-by-the-fire* with a part for Ellen and it was produced at the Duke of York's by Frohman. It also starred Helen Trevelyan, who had played 'Wendy' in the first *Peter Pan*. Ellen was 58 years old at the time and was in Birmingham touring *Alice*, when she learned of the death of her long-time stage partner Henry Irving. The good old trouper's 50 years in the theatre bore her through the performance that night, but could not carry her past the curtain line: 'I had a beautiful husband once . . .' and she broke down. The audience withheld their applause and quietly left the theatre.

Romance, 1915. Doris Keane (1881–1945) had a great success in E.B. Sheldon's *Romance* in the part of an Italian opera singer, at the Duke of York's. Another play to feature her was *Roxana*; in this scene she appears with Basil Sidney.

Wyndham's, 1899. One of the few West End theatres bearing an actor's name, Wyndham's was built to a design by W.G.R. Sprague on a plot of land between Charing Cross Road and St Martin's Lane, formerly owned by the Marquess of Salisbury. English-born Charles Wyndham, trained as a surgeon and a veteran of the American Civil War, had already been actor-manager at the Criterion for 22 years, and there met his future wife Mary Moore. Their monograms 'CW' and 'MM' appear in the decor at Wyndham's, where portraits of playwrights Goldsmith and Sheridan adorn the proscenium arch.

Charles Wyndham (1837–1919). The first play presented was a revival of *David Garrick* by Tom Robertson, with Wyndham in the name part. A revival of *Raffles*, and productions of Barrie's *Dear Brutus* and Sapper's *Bulldog Drummond* were among the highlights of Wyndham's reign. For six years from 1926, the thrillers of Edgar Wallace (p. 113), former crime reporter, drew the crowds.

Cynthia, 1904. This play by H.H. Davies, who wrote *Cousin Kate* (p. 70) was produced at Wyndham's with Gerald du Maurier (seated right) and Ethel Barrymore (seated second from left) in the leads. Miss Barrymore (1879–1959) was the sister of American actors John (p. 72) and Lionel, and crossed the Atlantic several times to appear in London plays.

Quiet Weekend at Wyndham's, 1940. Esther McCracken (left) wrote several very popular domestic comedies; *Quiet Wedding* was the first, produced in 1938, with *Quiet Weekend* (below) presented as a sequel two years later. Left to right: Glynis Johns as 'Miranda Bute', Michael Wilding as 'Denys Royd', Marjorie Fielding as his mother 'Mildred Royd' and Jeanne Stuart as 'Rowena Marriott'. The subject under discussion is Rowena's red trousers, the last straw for Mildred whose planned quiet weekend is threatened by a 20lb stolen salmon, a lost subscription to the church-organ fund, a frightful village concert, and worries about the love lives of her son Denys and daughter Mary. Esther McCracken began war service as a driver in the WRNS (Women's Royal Naval Service) and wrote *No Medals* about women on the home front.

The New (Albery), St Martin's Lane. Charles Wyndham had this theatre built in 1903 'back to back' and of similar design (both by Sprague) to his Wyndham's, then four years old. The name New was changed in 1977 to commemorate one-time director and Wyndham's stepson Sir Bronson Albery. Before the First World War, Fred Terry and his wife Julia Neilson took the New for nine successive six-month seasons. The 'Peter Pans' of Madge Titheradge, Unity Moore and Fay Compton flew there, and Noël Coward's first play *I'll Leave It to You* opened on 21 July 1920.

Old Vic at the New. Enemy bombs damaged Sadler's Wells (1940) and the Old Vic (1941) and the companies transferred to the New, where the drama company remained until 1950. The players listed in this programme include Harry Andrews, Peter Copley, Nicholas Hannen (Henry IV), Margaret Leighton, Miles Malleson, Laurence Olivier (Justice Shallow), Joyce Redman, Ralph Richardson (Sir John Falstaff), George Rose, Sydney Tafler and Sybil Thorndike (Mistress Quickly). Oscar Quitak, William Squire and Jane Wenham were among the supporting cast.

Gwen Ffrangcon Davies as 'Mary Stuart', September 1934. In the middle of a thick programme full of advertisements for ladies' tweed suits, ticket agencies, six new hats for ladies all at 20s, cruises on the Blue Star line, Cartier jewellery, Gleneagles Hotel, Haig's whiskey, Schweppe's table waters, Huntley and Palmer's biscuits . . . and W. Clarkson's fancy dress costumes (pp. 28 and 140) . . . I find the cast-list of *Queen of Scots* by Gordon Daviot. It includes Felix Aylmer, Glen Byam Shaw, Laurence Olivier ('Bothwell'), James Mason (doubling), George Howell, William Devlin and Ian Fleming; John Gielgud was the producer.

Bonnet over the Windmill, 1937. Playwright Dodie Smith had successes with *Autumn Crocus* (1931) and *Call it a Day* (1935) among others, before *Bonnet over the Windmill* was put on at the New. The plot involved Cecil Parker as actor-manager 'Sir Rupert Morellian' meeting a group of young untried actors. The romantic leads among them were played by James Mason and Anne Firth, standing in the doorway of the 'Essex windmill' of the title.

Autumn, 1938. Five years later, the St Martin's put on *Autumn* by Gregory Ratoff and Margaret Kennedy (her earlier work included *The Constant Nymph* at the New in 1925 with 21-year-old John Gielgud taking over the lead from 26-year-old Noël Coward). Left to right: Wyndham Goldie, Flora Robson and Jack Hawkins. The famous Ivy restaurant was once part of the St Martin's premises.

St Martin's, West Street. This theatre was intended as a 'twin' for the Ambassadors (next door but one), but was three years late opening, delayed by the First World War. Both theatres were designed by Sprague and initially leased by Charles B. Cochran. Modern plays such as Karel Capek's *R.U.R.* and *A Bill of Divorcement* by Clemence Dane were presented in the 1920s, and *The Wind and the Rain* opened on 18 October 1933. Its one set, seen here as 'the students' study on the first floor of Mrs McFie's boarding house in a Scottish university city' backed performances by Robert Harris, Margaret Moffat, Ivan Brandt and recent RADA student Celia Johnson, as 'Anne'.

The Ambassadors, West Street. This semi-subterranean theatre, seating 460 in a traditional interior (but with only one box at each level) opened in 1913 and saw the birth of Cochran's 'intimate revues', including French entertainers led by Alice Delysia. In 1921 Ivor Novello (p. 15) made his West End acting debut, and the same year the young Leslie Banks appeared in Lord Dunsany's *If*. This movie still is a reminder of his parallel career in films where, in the 1944 presentation of *Henry V*, he spoke the first and last words, as the Chorus standing in the Wooden O of the Globe Theatre, Bankside.

Jeanne de Casalis. In 1921 Jeanne de Casalis appeared with Ivor Novello at the Ambassadors. Three years later she was at that theatre again for *Fata Morgana*, in which Flora Robson (p. 109) had only her second West End role. The following year Miss de Casalis was in *Potiphar's Wife* at the Globe, causing a stir by appearing in pyjamas. In the Second World War this actress was one of those indomitable radio performers whose muddle-headed character 'Mrs Feather' raised many a smile in gloomy times.

JEANNE DE CASALIS

OWEN NARES
in
"TWO WHITE ARMS"
The New Comedy Farce
by Harold Dearden
at the
AMBASSADORS THEATRE

LEON M. LION'S PRODUCTION

Owen Nares (1888–1943). His good looks put him in the matinée idol category, and years would pass before he was cast in roles displaying his real talents. An early chance in Act Three of *Milestones* (p. 142) cast him opposite Gladys Cooper (1912), and the next year they were both in a revival of Sardou's *Diplomacy*. In *Two White Arms* he appeared with Sydney Fairbrother and Nigel Bruce (remembered by filmgoers as 'Doctor Watson' to Basil Rathbone's 'Sherlock Holmes'). Both *Robert's Wife* with Edith Evans in 1937 and *Rebecca* at the Queen's in 1940 gave Nares the chance to shine in deeper roles. The run of *Rebecca* came to an abrupt end when the theatre was badly damaged in an air-raid. He was last seen in *The Petrified Forest* at the Globe in 1942.

Vivien Leigh (1913–67). Miss Leigh, seen here as Titania in an Old Vic presentation of *A Midsummer Night's Dream* in 1938 – her 'wistful beauty and delicacy' winning praise from the *Theatre World* critic – made an early West End appearance at the Ambassadors in *The Mask of Virtue* (1935). She played 'Henriette', a young girl whose love for an evil roué (played by Ivor Novello) magically makes his ugly face as handsome as the mask behind which he hides. It was at a performance of this play that Laurence Olivier first set eyes on her: they married in August 1940.

Alan (A.P.) Herbert. His operetta *Riverside Nights* started life at the Lyric, Hammersmith, at the time of the general strike in 1926. It was transferred to the Ambassadors as audiences could more easily reach a central theatre. Sir Alan's musical plays, often with a sailing theme such as *The Water Gipsies*, have delighted generations of theatregoers.

Richard Goolden. Appearing in *Riverside Nights* was a young actor Richard Goolden, forever celebrated as Moley in *Toad of Toad Hall* (*Wind in the Willows*). He was also remembered for his many radio characterizations including the old night watchman: '. . . one night as I was sitting by my old fire-bucket . . .'.

The Cambridge, Earlham Street, Seven Dials. It is worth visiting the Cambridge simply to see the modern architecture and novel decor, and do not miss the gilded frieze of angularly athletic nude dancers in the foyer. *Charlot's Masquerade* opened the new theatre, one of six built in 1930. Later that year came *On the Spot*, an Edgar Wallace thriller, for which this was a publicity postcard. After the Second World War, the New London Opera Company spent two years at the Cambridge before going to Sadler's Wells (p. 128).

The Phoenix, Charing Cross Road. Another of the 1930 six, the Phoenix got off to a splendid start with the première of Noël Coward's *Private Lives*, in which he co-starred with Gertrude Lawrence (left), former pupil of Italia Conti (p. 20). They played ex-husband and wife 'Elyot' and 'Amanda'; Adrianne Allen and Laurence Olivier were the unfortunate second partners of the couple. In 1936 Noël and Gertie were together again at the Phoenix in *Tonight at 8.30*. In 1952 his *Quadrille* played there, with Alfred Lunt and Lynn Fontanne. It is hard to miss the nostalgic Noël Coward bar, opened in 1969, as it is in the Phoenix foyer.

The London Hippodrome. This theatre was built in 1900 on a prime site at the corner of Cranbourn Street, and started as a circus venue, symbolized by the horse and driver statue standing to this day at the top of the tower. Early on, the Hippodrome specialized in aquatic entertainment in, on or around its giant water tank, but after nine years the arena was converted into an auditorium, and music hall turns, ballet and revues took over. During the 1920s there were musical comedies like *Sunny* (1926) with Jack Buchanan (p. 126), *Hit the Deck* (1927) with Sydney Howard (p. 146) and *Mr Cinders* (1929) revived in 1983 at the Fortune.

Mobile advertisement. Harry Houdini (1873–1936), escapologist and illusionist, was one of the acts who appeared at the Hippodrome. A former locksmith, he claimed to be able to escape from any sealed trunk, tank of water, handcuffs, chains or bonds, which his audiences witnessed being applied.

Gordon Harker. He was the son of Joseph Harker, scenic designer at Daly's, the Garrick and elsewhere. One of young Gordon's early walk-on parts was as a Chinaman in *Kismet* (pp. 92–3), amid his father's scenery. He also acted as Fred Terry's prompter at one time. Between 1926 and 1931 he played in a number of Edgar Wallace thrillers at Wyndham's including *The Ringer* and *The Case of the Frightened Lady*. He appeared in many British films, and took the part of 'Police Constable George Dixon' when *The Blue Lamp* was dramatized at the Hippodrome.

Daly's, Leicester Square. American Augustin Daly had already been successful with his variety theatre on Broadway, and in the mid-1880s came to London, hoping to repeat the process. In his 'company of comedians' appearing at the old Strand Theatre in 1886 were Ada Rehan, Otis Skinner, Mrs G.H. Gilbert and John Drew. He teamed up with Irish-born George Edwardes of the Gaiety (p. 117) and opened in 1893 with *The Taming of the Shrew* at the new theatre on the corner of Cranbourn Street. On the right is part of the Hippodrome, on the opposite corner.

Maxine Elliott (1868–1940). She had been in Daly's New York company and came to London in 1895 to appear for him in *Two Gentlemen of Verona*. Her sister Gertrude (p. 21 – note the family likeness) married Johnston Forbes-Robertson. After her retirement from the American stage in 1914, Maxine came to England and worked for the war effort throughout the First World War. The headgear she is supporting here reminds me that (I'm told) when such large hats were fashionable, wearers in audiences were asked to remove them so those behind could see the stage. The hats were too big to hold all the time, so ladies would spike them to the padded back of the seat in front, using the murderously long hatpins they had just withdrawn.

Programme cover, *c.* 1894. *The Foresters* by Alfred Lord Tennyson, the first play to use electric light on stage, was one of the last joint presentations by Daly and Edwardes. When the latter became sole proprietor, his first production was Humperdinck's opera *Hansel and Gretel*, followed by programmes with actors such as Terriss, Forbes-Robertson, Ellen Terry and Sarah Bernhardt. In 1894 he began his successful run of musical comedies: *The Shop Girl, An Artist's Model, The Geisha, The Runaway Girl*, and so on.

George Edwardes (1852–1915). 'The Guv'nor' was in charge of the Gaiety theatres from 1886 until his death, as well as being at Daly's. Among his stars were Seymour Hicks, George Grossmith Junior, Edmund Payne, Ada Reeve, Marie Tempest, Lottie Venne, Rutland Barrington and C. Hayden Coffin.

HUNTLEY WRIGHT.

Huntley Wright. This comedian was another of Edwardes' regular team, and he could sing and dance as well. In *San Toy* (1899) he sang 'Chinee Soldier Man', and 'Chick Chick Chick' in *A Country Girl* (1902) (p. 121). He was still going strong in 1921 when Daly's presented *Sybil* – 347 performances, in which he starred with José Collins and Harry Welchman.

The Cingalee, 1905. This play at Daly's ran for 363 performances with C. Hayden Coffin (p. 47) as 'Charles Vereker' and Sybil Arundale as 'Nunoya'. Miss Arundale was a versatile actress; we find her in 1925 playing at the St James's in a revival of Ibsen's *The Wild Duck* and, three years later, she was partly responsible for establishing a small try-out theatre, the Embassy, in Hampstead.

Two leading dancers. Principal dancer at the Empire, Leicester Square, for ten years from 1897, Danish Adeline Genée (left) was rehearsing at Daly's when George Edwardes rose from his seat in the stalls and demonstrated how he would like her to dance. This was for an appearance in *The Little Michus*, the play advertised in tall letters along the theatre's roofline on page 116. It ran for nearly 400 performances in 1905. Topsy Sinden (right) appeared at Daly's as 'Trixie' in *San Toy* (scenery credited to Joseph Harker) in 1899. Edwardes at one time owned a racehorse named after the play. Topsy Sinden was a graceful 'thistledown' type of dancer; she was 30 years old when appointed principal dancer at the Empire, Leicester Square, in 1907, to succeed Genée.

The Merry Widow, 1907. Franz Lehar's music, the glamorous cast, lavish settings and stunning costumes made this the greatest of Edwardes' successes at Daly's. It ran for 778 performances and saved 'The Guv'nor', whose fortunes had taken a bad turn. The principal actors to the fore in this scene from the second act are (left to right) George Graves, Lily Elsie, Joseph Coyne, Robert Evett, Mary Grey and W.H. Berry. It shows a dramatic moment during a party at the Paris embassy of the state of 'Pontevedro', given by its wealthiest citizen, 'Anna Glavari', the merry widow.

Lily Elsie as the 'Merry Widow'. She had already appeared at the Gaiety and the old Strand, before her triumph as 'Anna Glavari'. Lehar's music – the *Merry Widow Waltz*, songs 'Velia', 'You'll Find Me at Maxim's', 'Women, Women, Women' and 'Driving in the Park with You' – has been sung, whistled and played for almost 90 years. With some of the beautiful costumes designed for her, Miss Elsie wore hats with wide, curving brims which set a fashion.

Postcard publicity for a play at Daly's. *A Country Girl*, composed by Lionel Monckton, was one of George Edwardes' many musical comedies presented during his 20-year reign at the theatre. The show opened in January 1902 and ran for 729 performances, and is considered by many to be the finest of some twelve he staged.

The Lady of the Rose, 1922. Edwardes died in 1915, but the tradition of musical comedy at Daly's was maintained by Oscar Asche (p. 92). After *The Maid of the Mountains* he presented *The Lady of the Rose* with Phyllis Dare in the dual role of 'the Countess Mariana' and a portrait come to life. Harry Welchman – handsome hero of so many other plays before and after – as 'Colonel Bolivar', commandeering Mariana's castle and casting his eyes over her, was for once the villain of the piece: ' . . . he thinks more of a horse than he does of a man, and carries a whip with him everywhere!' Seated, left to right, are Winnie Collins as 'Rosina', the maid, Phyllis Dare, and Ivy Tresmand as 'Sophie Lavalle', leader of the ballet. Standing, left to right, Harry Welchman, Leonard Mackay as 'The Baron' and ballet-master, Noel Leyland as 'Count Adrian' and Huntley Wright (p. 118) as the silhouette-cutter 'Suitangi'. Music for the play was by Jean Gilbert, lyrics by Harry Graham, and Frederick Lonsdale wrote the libretto, as he did for *Madame Pompadour* at Daly's in 1923.

Evelyn Laye (b. 1900). After early
appearances in Brighton, at the Gaiety
and for C.B. Cochran at the Pavilion,
'Boo' Laye came to Daly's in 1923 for a
revival of *The Merry Widow* (opposite
Carl Brisson in the Joseph Coyne part of
'Count Danilo'), followed by *Madame
Pompadour* with Derek Oldham and
Bertram Wallis. In 1925 she starred less
successfully in *Cleopatra* (music by
Oscar Strauss). Elsewhere she played in
The Dollar Princess, Bitter Sweet and
Lilac Time, opened the Piccadilly
Theatre in 1923 in *Blue Eyes*, and was a
stunning principal boy for a number of
pantomimes. As a comedy actress she
appeared in the long-running *No Sex
Please, We're British* which opened in
1971.

KENETH KENT
IN ST HELENA
DALY'S THEATRE 1936

Keneth Kent. Versatile actor-producer-
playwright-adaptor Kent attended the Royal
Academy of Dramatic Art, to which he
returned to teach in the mid-1930s. He made
his first London appearance aged 20 in
1912. When *The Constant Nymph* was
produced at the New in 1926, he created the
part of 'Jacob Birnbaum', and appeared in
the same role in a revival. In 1935 the Old
Vic staged *St Helena* in which he played
Napoleon; it transferred to Daly's in
November 1936 – one of the last plays seen
there, before the theatre's closure the
following year, with subsequent demolition
and building on the site of the Warner
cinema.

The Alhambra, 24–7 Leicester Square, 1874. The Moorish-style Royal Panopticon of Science and Art opened in Leicester Square in 1854, but was soon renamed the Alhambra. Several changes of entertainment, title and seating took place before a fire destroyed it in December 1882. It was rebuilt on similar lines but without the minaret-like towers. It was included as one of the sights of London in a set of French stereoscope cards, with Turkish baths next door!

The Devil's Forge, 1903. The Alhambra had various links with the ballet world. Monsieur Léotard (the great trapeze artist and inventor of the one-piece garment worn by dancers) performed at the original theatre in 1861. The rebuilt theatre specialized in spectacular ballet presentations (as above) and in 1911, 1919 and 1931 Diaghilev's Ballet Russes appeared there.

BALLROOM SCENE FROM THE ALHAMBRA SUCCESS "WALTZES FROM VIENN

Waltzes from Vienna at the Alhambra. Nothing objectionable about this spectacular musical play! – let us hope everyone had forgotten when scandalized authorities withdrew the old theatre's licence after a performance of the can-can. . . . In 1914, at a Sunday concert for soldiers, singer Sybil Vane gave the first performance of 'Keep the Home Fires Burning', accompanied at the Alhambra piano by the composer, Ivor Novello, aged 21.

The Bing Boys are Here, 1916. This was the first musical play in which George Robey (right) appeared, though he had been on the halls as a comedian for 25 years before that. Partnered by Alfred Lester (left) and with songs like 'If You Were the Only Girl in the World', 'I stopped – I Looked – I Listened' and 'The Kipling Walk', he was a great wartime success. In his sixties, he turned his talents to drama, playing Sir John Falstaff in *Henry IV* in 1935, and in Laurence Olivier's film of *Henry V* 18 years later. The Odeon cinema was built on the site of the Alhambra, which closed in 1936.

Jack Buchanan (1890–1957). This Scottish actor made an early London appearance at the Alhambra in one of the first André Charlot revues. In 1921, he introduced Ivor Novello's song 'And Her Mother Came Too' in Charlot's *A to Z*. His charm, humour and elegance brought him many West End roles. He was actor-manager at the Garrick after the Second World War. When Ivor Novello died in 1950 while playing in *King's Rhapsody* at the Palace, Jack took over his friend's leading role – perhaps the most distressing part he ever had to perform.

The Empire, Leicester Square. A theatre stood on this site for almost 150 years, with music-hall dominating the Edwardian era; ballet was led by Adeline Genée and Topsy Sinden (p. 119). *Razzle Dazzle* was a patriotic revue in 1916 produced by Albert de Courville, who put on similar spectacles at the Hippodrome (p. 114). Later came *The Lilac Domino, Irene, The Rebel Maid* and *Lady be Good* with Adèle and Fred Astaire, and Sybil Thorndike's production of *Henry VIII*. It was rebuilt in 1928 as a picture house, and the present Empire cinema dates from 1963.

The Dominion, Tottenham Court Road. The theatre had not long been opened when this photograph was taken: *Silver Wings*, a musical adapted from the 1920s American drama *The Broken Wing* about an aeroplane crash, was only its second play (1929–30).

The Lon Chaney 1925 silent movie of *The Phantom of the Opera* with added dialogue followed *Silver Wings*, and in 1931 George V saw Charlie Chaplin in the movie *City Lights*. The site of the Dominion had once been occupied by a leper hospital and later by a brewery. Pasquale Troise and his Mandoliers, heard on radio, records and at restaurants like Quaglino's, were featured during one of the Dominion's periods as a variety theatre.

Sadler's Wells (see Old Vic, pp. 62–6). The site was originally exactly that: medicinal springs, where Mr Sadler set up a pleasure garden. Various names, uses, rebuildings and almost 250 years later – years that saw Grimaldi the clown perform, naval battles re-enacted as 'aquatic drama', skaters, boxers and Mr Phelps' Shakespearean company perform – Lilian Baylis's new theatre opened on the site. From 1934 to 1946 (apart from Second World War closure and bomb damage) opera and ballet were staged; left is a scene from *Wedding Bouquet* (1938) with Robert Helpmann and Margaret Dale.

Section Five

SHAFTESBURY AVENUE

The Piccadilly, 1941. This large theatre opened in Denman Street in 1928. Only one play, Blue
Eyes *with Evelyn Laye, was staged before the Piccadilly went over to showing the new 'talkie'
films, but drama and musical comedy soon resumed. Cecil Parker and Fay Compton (above)
appeared in Noël Coward's* Blithe Spirit *with Kay Hammond and Margaret Rutherford in 1941,
but not long after John Gielgud's production of* Macbeth *there, the curse of the Scottish play
struck when a flying bomb damaged the theatre.*

Rainbow Corner. Only a few steps from the Piccadilly, the building known in the Second World War as 'Rainbow Corner' contained a canteen, information desk and entertainment facilities for United States servicemen who found themselves in the capital. It was calculated that volunteers worked a total of 184,358 hours between 11 November 1942 and 10 December 1944.

Beatrice Lillie (1898–1985). The Canadian-born entertainer, Lady Robert Peel off-stage, was one of the theatre folk, great and small, who made their contribution to the war effort by going with ENSA (p. 18) to give shows to the forces in camps and on active service, as well as visiting factories.

The Lyric. As the nineteenth century neared its end, the geographic centre of theatreland began to move westward. Shaftesbury Avenue, from Piccadilly Circus to Cambridge Circus, eventually had six theatres, starting with Mr Henry Leslie's Lyric in 1888. The cover of the programme (left) with its classical allusions to the theatre's name, was for *Florodora*, seen on Tuesday 9 January 1900 by the original owner 'with Tom and Edie'. The play's plot concerns a perfume of that name; J. Grossmith and Son's advertisement (right) alongside the cast list speaks for itself. Leslie Stuart's song 'Tell me, Pretty Maiden' has been revived frequently for Royal Variety shows and other charity occasions, as the means of including considerable numbers of actors and actresses in a single scene.

The Three Musketeers, 1909. Lewis Waller first presented this play in 1898 at the Globe, starring as 'd'Artagnan', with Gerald Gurney as 'Aramis', Bassett Roe as 'Athos' and Charles Goodheart as 'Porthos'. In the 1909 Lyric revival, Mr Waller (left) and Mr Roe (arm in sling) repeated their original roles, but Shiel Barry (second left) was 'Aramis' and Herbert Jarman (right) was 'Porthos'. By all accounts, this was a truly romantic, thrilling swashbuckler of a play.

The Duchess of Dantzig. Evie Greene, who had played the leading character of 'Dolores' in *Florodora* at the Lyric in 1900, returned three years later for this costume piece.

The Apollo. Close to the Lyric, the Apollo (above) has an attractive façade which is worth viewing from across Shaftesbury Avenue. Closer inspection will find the lucky mascot of the first owner Henry Lowenfield, incorporating two lions and a lizard, carved beside the main doors. The Apollo opened in 1901 as a musical comedy theatre, and Edward German's *Tom Jones* (below) upheld that ideal. It was presented in 1907 by Robert Courtneidge who, at one time or another, had plays in nearly every Shaftesbury Avenue theatre, and it marked his daughter Cicely's debut in London, where she was still delighting audiences more than 60 years later.

Left to Right   CAROL DEXTER, AUDREY BOYES,
(Front Row)   PAT DENNY, EILEEN McCARTHY

(Back Row)   PEGGY HAMILTON, JOAN CLARKSON

Idiot's Delight. Robert Emmet Sherwood's plays before the Second World War such as *The Petrified Forest* (1935) and *Idiot's Delight* (1936) – which was awarded the Pulitzer Prize for Drama – sought to warn the world of the devastation to come. *Idiot's Delight* told of a party of travelling players marooned in the cocktail lounge of a hotel 'on a mountain peak in the continent of Europe'. It was made into a movie with the dubious distinction of starring Clark Gable as a song and dance man. The play was at the Apollo in 1938, with Raymond Massey (father of Anna and Daniel) returning to the theatre where he had made his West End debut 16 years before, starring as 'Harry Van' (right above) with Franklin Dyall as 'Doctor Waldersee'. The young ladies (left) played the dancers of the company.

Phyllis Neilson Terry, 1922. As her name suggests, she was the daughter of Fred Terry and Julia Neilson; her brother Dennis was also an actor, and they were cousins of John Gielgud. Phyllis appeared in the revival of *Trilby* at the Apollo in 1922, and in a new play *The Wheel* by J.B. Fagan, of the Royal Court, who a few years later wrote *And So to Bed*, the play about Samuel Pepys.

Seymour Hicks (1871–1949). One of the few actors to have a theatre bearing his name, he was knighted in 1935 after nearly 50 years as actor, manager and playwright. He made his debut, aged 16, at the Grand, Islington and staged the first-ever revue in London, only six years later. He was associated with Daly's and the Aldwych before opening the Hicks in 1906, on the corner of Shaftesbury Avenue and Rupert Street. It was designed by W.G.R. Sprague as one of a matching pair, like his Strand and Aldwych theatres. The twin of the Hicks (renamed the Globe in 1909) was the Queen's, on the corner of Wardour Street. One would not realize this now, as the façade of the latter had to be rebuilt after Second World War bombing.

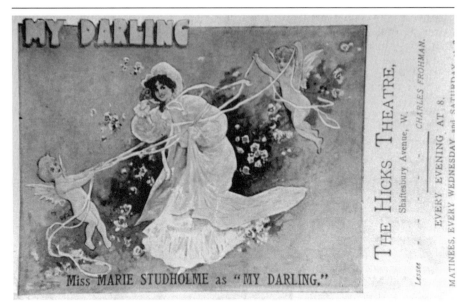

MY DARLING

Miss MARIE STUDHOLME as "MY DARLING."

THE HICKS THEATRE,
Shaftesbury Avenue, W.
CHARLES FROHMAN.
EVERY EVENING AT 8.
MATINEES, EVERY WEDNESDAY and SATURDAY
Lessee

Seymour Hicks and his theatre. The rare advertising postcard (above) caught the theatre in the short spell under its original name of the Hicks. Marie Studholme (p. 83) was another actress who appeared on many postcards in many contrived settings, always with a brilliant smile.

Mrs Seymour Hicks was Ellaline Terriss, daughter of Breezy Bill (p. 43); she introduced the song 'The Honeysuckle and the Bee' in *Bluebell in Fairyland*, one of several plays in which she and her husband appeared together. They were among the first players to go to France to entertain the troops in the First World War. In 1994, to general approval, the theatre was once again given an actor's name: it is now the Gielgud.

Brewster's Millions, 1907. The Hicks had only a year to wait for its first hit show which was *Brewster's Millions* starring Gerald du Maurier, fresh from his triumph as 'Raffles' at the Comedy (p. 78).

A Waltz Dream. This operetta starring Gertie Millar and George Grossmith, with music by Oscar Strauss, came to the Hicks in 1908, a year after its first performance in Vienna. Miss Millar as 'Frantzi Steingruber' stands at the top of the steps, with Robert Evett (left, looking towards her) as 'Lieutenant Niki'.

The Hon Phil. Following *A Waltz Dream* in October 1908, in the cast of this 'musical piece' was Elsie Spain (far left) as 'Brigette', G.P. Huntley (p. 83) (centre in light jacket) as 'the Hon Phil Gifford' and Denise Orme (right in long gown) as 'Marie'.

Peg o' my Heart. This play had already numbered 710 performances at the Comedy when it went to the Globe in 1916 – and that, after almost as long a triumphant start in New York. It originally starred American Laurette Taylor (whose husband John Hartley Manners wrote the play for her). A.E. Matthews (affectionately 'Matty' to everyone), with a clown and a Christy minstrel in his ancestry, cornered the market in dear old ditherers in British plays and movies, after many years in farce and light comedy – he was over 90 when he died.

Tuesday Evening, February 21st.
MR. LEWIS WALLER IN
" BARDELYS THE MAGNIFICENT,"
The Cast includes
Miss Lottie Venne, Miss Madge Titheradge, Mr. Wm. Haviland.
At the **GLOBE THEATRE**, Shaftesbury Avenue, W.

Lewis Waller's later plays. Waller played more than 200 different parts in his 32 years on the stage. He excelled in Shakespearean roles; hearing his passionate voice, recorded in Henry V's Harfleur speech some 80 years ago, one can well believe it. His admirers, however, preferred him in more melodramatic parts, and *Bardelys the Magnificent* (top) and *A Butterfly on the Wheel* (bottom), a 1911 divorce/courtroom drama were among those he played in later years.

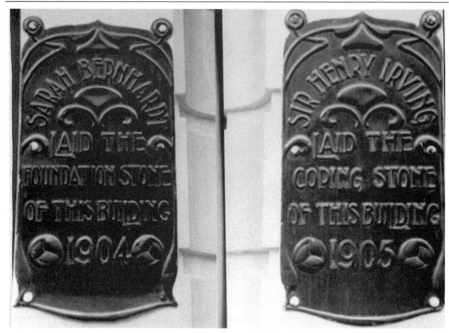

Clarkson's, 41–3 Wardour Street. Such was the reputation of Clarkson's wigs and costumes in Wellington Street (p. 28) that leading stage figures Sarah Bernhardt and Henry Irving were involved with the building of new premises in Wardour Street. These evocative panels can still be seen. Willy Clarkson is said to have been the inspiration for the character of 'Madame Lucy', the male fashion designer in *Irene* (1920), a role created by Robert Hale, father of Binnie (p. 145) and Sonnie.

Suzette, 1917. For more than 250 performances Mlle Gaby Deslys, the glamorous French star, decorated the stage of the Globe in her farewell role. Harry Pilcer shared this scene with her. Peacock feathers might have looked better in her head-dress, but it is a theatrical tradition that they are never used on stage (an extension of a general superstition). This tradition had been flouted in an earlier Globe production which closed after only 13 performances.

Emlyn Williams (1905–87). The celebrated Welsh actor, playwright and producer, appeared in the opening play at the Duchess, not long after his London debut in 1927. Following his own *Night Must Fall* and *The Corn is Green* at the same theatre, he brought *The Light of Heart* (1941) and *The Morning Star* (1942) to the Globe. He had several successes in Shakespearean roles, notably Shylock and Iago in 1956, but thereafter was often seen in his solo performances with readings from Charles Dickens and Dylan Thomas, worldwide.

Rupert Street, W1, 1950. On the side wall of the Globe (far right) is an advertisement for *Ring Round the Moon*, the very successful adaptation by Christopher Fry from the French of Jean Anouilh's *L'Invitation au Château*. It opened on 26 January 1950, directed by Peter Brook with scenery designed by Oliver Messel (p. 26, 18 years earlier). Margaret Rutherford played 'Madame Desmermortes', with Paul Schofield in the dual role of her twin nephews 'Hugo' and 'Frederic'. Others in the cast were David Horne (p. 41, 22 years earlier), Claire Bloom, William Mervyn, Cecil Trouncer, Richard Wattis and Mona Washbourne.

The Royalty. Though a modern theatre of this name has existed since 1960 as part of an office block on the site of the old Stoll, this Royalty is the one that stood in Dean Street from 1840 to 1955. It staged the first joint effort of Gilbert and Sullivan with *Trial by Jury* in 1875, and pioneered several 'new' writers like Shaw, Ibsen and O'Casey. *Milestones* (left) by Arnold Bennett and Edward Knoblock (of *Kismet*, p. 93) was first produced in 1912. A performance was given before George V. The cast included Dennis Eadie and Mary Jerrold (pictured) and Lionel Atwill, Owen Nares and Gladys Cooper. It was the three-act story of a family, set in 1860, 1885 and 1914. The reality of 1914 was shown in *Home on Leave* (right). The postcard advertising the play was sent in January 1918 to 'Brother George' by 'Jack' who was on leave.

The Queen's, 1909. Although the Queen's is an attractive theatre (behind its 1959 façade is a rebuilding of the blitzed original) and has had its share of successes and flops, good and bad performances, I find only one photograph in my collection to feature it. This was an early offering, when H.B. Irving took over management after the theatre opened, of *The Lyons Mail*. With him in this scene is his off-stage wife Dorothea Baird (the first 'Trilby' at Her Majesty's in 1895 – p. 69).

The Palace, Cambridge Circus. In 1891 Richard D'Oyly Carte, flushed with the success of his Savoy operas by Gilbert and Sullivan, built the Royal English Opera House, facing Cambridge Circus with Shaftesbury Avenue on one side (left) and Old Compton Street, with a view through to the site of the Prince Edward (London Casino) on the other.

Sir Arthur Sullivan. He responded to the building of the opera house with a single work called *Ivanhoe*. Shortly afterwards D'Oyly Carte sold out to Augustus Harris, who renamed it the Palace Theatre of Varieties. Sullivan died in 1900 and his monument stands in the Embankment Gardens.

Anna Pavlova (1881–1931). In 1910, after some time with Diaghilev's troupe, she made her London debut at the Palace, presented by Alfred Butt who brought revue to the West End. She made her home in London whence, before and after the First World War, she took her ballets on tour throughout the world. Her famous solo *The Dying Swan*, arranged for her by Mikhail Fokine to Saint-Saëns' music, may owe something to the dancing of Isadora Duncan (p. 76) who first visited Russia in 1905.

The Co-optimists, 1924. This pierrot troupe 'that never saw the seaside' was a group of artists brought together by the gimmick of their costumes and format. They included Stanley Holloway (far left) and Davy Burnaby (fourth from left, with monocle). Laddie Cliff and Melville Gideon were others who performed with the group. They appeared at various West End theatres in the 1920s, and were at the Palace in 1924.

Binnie Hale (1900–84). In this 1932 advertisement she is endorsing Columbia radio-gramophones: 32 guineas (£33 2s 0d) or twelve monthly payments of £2 14s 0d. Seven years earlier, she had appeared in *No, No Nanette* at the Palace. Presented by Herbert Clayton and Jack Waller, the Vincent Youmans musical also starred George Grossmith and Joseph Coyne (from *The Merry Widow*, pp. 120–1).

Oh, Letty!, 1938. Clayton and Waller continued to present hit shows at the Palace with *Mercenary Mary, The Girl Friend* and *Hit the Deck* among them. Sydney Howard (left of microphone) starred in *Oh, Letty!*, a modern-dress musical. Also in the cast were Phyllis Stanley as 'Letty', a Hollywood film star, and Wylie Watson as 'Chester', the timid butt of all the goings-on. Howard and Watson both appeared in British movies. The Palace has a splendidly restored interior; the downstairs bar and restaurant in particular are the Edwardian era reincarnated.

E.S. Willard at the Shaftesbury, 1888–1941. A fire station now occupies the site of the first Shaftesbury, designed by Phipps and seating some 1,200. It faced the south side of the Palace across Shaftesbury Avenue, and opened with Johnston Forbes-Robertson in *As You Like It*. Willard (1853–1915), a specialist in villains in Victorian melodramas, took over management very soon, producing the plays of Henry Arthur Jones. Robert Courtneidge (p. 133) assumed the management in 1909.

The Arcadians, 1909. Courtneidge opened his management of the Shaftesbury with this musical comedy by Lionel Monckton and Howard Talbot. Left to right, above: Harry Welchman ('Jack Meadows'), Florence Smithson ('Sombra'), Phyllis Dare ('Eileen Cavanagh') and Nelson 'Bunch' Keys ('Bobby'). Others in the cast were Alfred Lester, Courtneidge's daughter Cicely, and Dan Rolyat seen below as 'James Smith' amid the maidens of Arcadia.

Another picture of *The Arcadians*. Act Two was set at Ascot races, to which the Arcadian hero had been banished for telling a lie. As can happen only in musical comedy, he finds himself on a galloping racehorse.

Princess Caprice, 1912. This was seen by George V on 15 August 1912 and was another of Courtneidge's productions at the Shaftesbury which, after more than 50 years' entertaining its patrons, was totally destroyed in an air-raid in April 1941. The wide range of entertainment presented included Harry Lauder in *Three Cheers!* (1920), Clemence Dane's *Will Shakespeare* (1921), a thriller *The Cat and the Canary* and a farce *Tons of Money* (both 1922), and the nautical comedy *The Middle Watch* (1929).

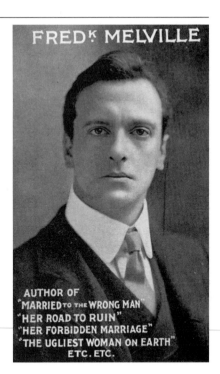

FRED^k MELVILLE

AUTHOR OF
"MARRIED TO THE WRONG MAN"
"HER ROAD TO RUIN"
"HER FORBIDDEN MARRIAGE"
"THE UGLIEST WOMAN ON EARTH"
ETC. ETC.

The Prince's, Shaftesbury Avenue. At the very top of Shaftesbury Avenue, the Bertie Crewe-designed theatre known today as the Shaftesbury was from its opening on Boxing Day 1911 until 1963 called the Prince's, the name chosen by Fred Melville and his brother Walter when they moved from the Lyceum (p. 25).

PRINCES THEATRE, SHAFTESBURY AVENUE (New Oxford Street End.
Every Evening at 7·30.   Matinees, Wed. Thurs. & Sat. at 2·30.
POPULAR PRICES. 5/. to 6d.   Seats Reserved from 2/6
Phone No. 5983 Gerrard.   THE GREAT DRAMA   Box Office 10 till 10
"ON HIS MAJESTY'S SERVICE"

"Daddy's Come Home."

This postcard advertisement, sent in February 1915, speaks for itself, as the Melvilles applied melodrama to the First World War.

Alf's Button, Prince's, 1924. W.A. Darlington, author and distinguished drama critic of the *Daily Telegraph*, turned his book *Alf's Button* into 'an extravaganza in three acts' (Act One being the devastated area behind the British lines), which ran for 111 performances. It concerned Alf, a soldier in the trenches, whose buttons are made from Aladdin's lamp recycled; when he polishes them the genie appears, offering the customary three wishes.

Bird's eye view of Aldwych and Kingsway. The two roads radiating like a V to the top of the photograph are Drury Lane (left) and Kingsway (right). The open square in the top right-hand corner is Lincoln's Inn Fields and the white-edged block between the Fields and Kingsway opened in 1911 as the London Opera House. After only five years it became the Stoll picture house, named after Sir Oswald Stoll of the London Coliseum. During the Second World War it reverted to use as a theatre and from then on had revues, pantomimes, revivals of musicals like *The Student Prince* and *Rose Marie*, ice-shows, ballet and opera. It closed with *Titus Andronicus* with Laurence Olivier and Vivien Leigh and was demolished in 1957.

The Kingsway. There was a theatre in Great Queen Street from 1882 until 1956, first known as the Novelty. It staged the English première of *A Doll's House* by Ibsen in 1889. After rebuilding, in 1907, it acquired its present title and Lena Ashwell as actor-manager. Already well-known for appearances in *Mrs Dane's Defence* and *Madame X*, she put on *The Sway Boat* (above) by Wilfred T. Coleby, 'the study of a modern neurotic woman'. Left to right: E.W. Garden, Frances Ivor, Dennis Eadie (as 'Lord Kilross'). Granville Barker and Lilah McCarthy (p. 40), Barry Jackson and Sir Donald Wolfit all played at the Kingsway, which was demolished after Second World War bombing.

All the Leading Actors & Actresses
WILL BE PRESENT AT THE
Theatrical Garden Party
in aid of the ACTORS' ORPHANAGE
Monday, June 6th, 1932
His Royal Highness PRINCE GEORGE, has graciously consented to be present

Tickets : **3/- before** the day, at all Theatres and Agencies. **5/- on** the day

ROYAL BOTANICAL GARDENS
(Inner Circle) REGENT'S PARK, N.W.

Theatrical Garden Party. The Kingsway's programme dated 9 May 1932 (when the Representative English Players presented Oliver Goldsmith's *She Stoops to Conquer* with Clare Greet, Mary Merral and Valentine Dyall) included this advertisement, which speaks for itself. HRH Prince George was the Duke of Kent, who in 1934 married Princess Marina of Greece.

The Royal Princess. Bert Coote's production of *The Fatal Wedding* was presented at the second Oxford Street theatre on the site opposite Poland Street. Macready, Fanny Kemble, Henry Irving and Ellen Terry (in her debut aged nine) (p. 10) had all acted in the earlier theatre. Edwin Booth opened the new building in 1880 with *Hamlet*. It was his younger brother John who assassinated the United States President Abraham Lincoln. The building was demolished in 1931, having given its last show nearly 30 years earlier.

Harry Tate (1872–1940). He made his debut at the Oxford Music Hall, on the corner of Oxford Street and Tottenham Court Road, in 1895. His real surname was Hutchinson; he claimed inspiration for 'Tate' from the time he worked in the sugar refinery of that name. His comical trademarks were a high-pitched explosive way of speaking, and his hilarious sketches based on the human failings of those who went 'Fishing', 'Golfing' or ' Motoring'.

Two more 'Peter Pans'. Gladys Cooper (above) played 'Peter' for two seasons in 1923 and 1924, when in her thirties and managing the Playhouse (p. 50). Franklyn Dyall (p. 134) and Ian Hunter were her 'Captain Hooks'. Nova Pilbeam (below) was a child actress in plays such as *Toad of Toad Hall* before Gaumont-British films claimed her. She was 'Peter' in 1935 at the age of 16, to George Hayes's 'Captain Hook', at the London Palladium, Argyll Street.

Tottenham Court Road. The Scala, built in 1905 near Goodge Street as a successor to the Bancroft's Prince of Wales (p. 82), had a chequered career and is chiefly remembered now as Second World War headquarters of a United States Army entertainments group, as the venue for several seasons of *Peter Pan*, and for amateur productions. In December 1954, Lloyds Bank Operatic and Dramatic Society presented their annual show. A rehearsal is seen here (above) with (left to right) Jean Pym, Joan Perrott, Jean Prior, Valerie Richards, Dorothy Waring, Ray Thackeray, Pauline Edwards and Annette Rouse. Below is a scene from their production of *No, No, Nanette*.

Ben Greet (1857–1936). He began producing Shakespeare out of doors in 1886, coming to Regent's Park with his Woodland Players some 14 years later, and to the grounds of the Crystal Palace thereafter. He also toured the United Kingdom and America, and a number of leading actors had their start in his companies. In 1914 he helped establish the Old Vic and, between that winter and spring 1918, directed more than 20 Shakespeare plays. He was a pioneer in taking play productions to schools, and was knighted in 1929. In my collection I have a copy of a somewhat tetchy 'open letter' he wrote to the people of Seaford, Sussex (where he had a regular summer season), chiding them for engaging a rival company while he was out of the country.

Regent's Park. In 1933 a permanent theatre was built in the park, after Sydney Carroll revived Ben Greet's idea. From 1939 to 1961 it was run by Robert Atkins, Shakespearean actor and Greet's successor as director at the Old Vic. This is a scene from *A Midsummer Night's Dream* in June 1938.

Griffith Jones and Margaretta Scott in *Romeo and Juliet*, Regent's Park Open Air Theatre.

The Globe, Bankside. The twentieth-century interpretation of William Shakespeare's theatre is nearing completion as this book goes to print. It will add an exciting element to the diversity of London's theatres, already so rich and varied in architecture and decor, in history of plays and players, and the audiences who have been to see them. The opening of a new London theatre, even if it is an echo of an old one, is a memorable event. I hope that the more recent photographs in this book have inspired enjoyable reminiscences for my readers, while the older ones have intrigued them with all that went on in the distant past.

Acknowledgements

Warmest thanks go to the following, for help with contents of the book: Glynne Miller, Diana Howard, Sheila Palk, John Grice, Geoff Robinson (of The White Horse, Rupert Street, W1), Paul Savident, Graham Tubb, Pat Doyle of the British Banjo Circle, Fred Bates, the late Mrs Florrie Armes (gift of old programmes), the late Mrs Billy Dean (gift of old prints), staff of the Theatre Museum Study Room, Covent Garden, WC2, staff of Boot's, Seaford, and the processing laboratory, Rupert Harding and Anne Bennett of Alan Sutton Publishing Limited for editing and general encouragement, and friends and colleagues for advice and constructive criticism.

Though I have absorbed much of the information in these pages over the years and researched each addition to my collection of photographs, facts and (especially) dates have to be checked. As well as those quoted in the text, books consulted include: *Concise Companion to the Theatre* (edited by Phyllis Hartnoll) (Omega, 1972), *William Terriss and Richard Prince* by George Rowell (Society for Theatre Research, 1987), *Confessions of an Actor* by Laurence Olivier (Coronet, 1982), *Present Indicative* by Noël Coward (Heinemann, 1947), and *The Lost Theatres of London* by R. Mander and J. Mitchenson (New English Library, 1975).

None of the pictures reproduced appears to be under copyright, but the current practice of marketing photographic copies means the original details on their backs are not available. Apologies are rendered for any source not fully cleared or acknowledged; a note to the publishers in such case will ensure an amendment in any reprint.

BRITAIN IN OLD PHOTOGRAPHS

To order any of these titles please telephone Littlehampton Book Services on 01903 721596

ALDERNEY

Alderney: A Second Selection, *B Bonnard*

BEDFORDSHIRE

Bedfordshire at Work, *N Lutt*

BERKSHIRE

Maidenhead, *M Hayles & D Hedges*
Around Maidenhead, *M Hayles & B Hedges*
Reading, *P Southerton*
Reading: A Second Selection, *P Southerton*
Sandhurst and Crowthorne, *K Dancy*
Around Slough, *J Hunter & K Hunter*
Around Thatcham, *P Allen*
Around Windsor, *B Hedges*

BUCKINGHAMSHIRE

Buckingham and District, *R Cook*
High Wycombe, *R Goodearl*
Around Stony Stratford, *A Lambert*

CHESHIRE

Cheshire Railways, *M Hitches*
Chester, *S Nichols*

CLWYD

Clwyd Railways, *M Hitches*

CLYDESDALE

Clydesdale, *Lesmahagow Parish Historical Association*

CORNWALL

Cornish Coast, *T Bowden*
Falmouth, *P Gilson*
Lower Fal, *P Gilson*
Around Padstow, *M McCarthy*
Around Penzance, *J Holmes*
Penzance and Newlyn, *J Holmes*
Around Truro, *A Lyne*
Upper Fal, *P Gilson*

CUMBERLAND

Cockermouth and District, *J Bernard Bradbury*
Keswick and the Central Lakes, *J Marsh*
Around Penrith, *F Boyd*
Around Whitehaven, *H Fancy*

DERBYSHIRE

Derby, *D Buxton*
Around Matlock, *D Barton*

DEVON

Colyton and Seaton, *T Gosling*
Dawlish and Teignmouth, *G Gosling*
Devon Aerodromes, *K Saunders*
Exeter, *P Thomas*
Exmouth and Budleigh Salterton, *T Gosling*
From Haldon to Mid-Dartmoor, *T Hall*
Honiton and the Otter Valley, *J Yallop*
Around Kingsbridge, *K Tanner*
Around Seaton and Sidmouth, *T Gosling*
Seaton, Axminster and Lyme Regis, *T Gosling*

DORSET

Around Blandford Forum, *B Cox*
Bournemouth, *M Colman*
Bridport and the Bride Valley, *J Burrell & S Humphries*
Dorchester, *T Gosling*
Around Gillingham, *P Crocker*

DURHAM

Darlington, *G Flynn*
Darlington: A Second Selection, *G Flynn*
Durham People, *M Richardson*
Houghton-le-Spring and Hetton-le-Hole, *K Richardson*
Houghton-le-Spring and Hetton-le-Hole:
  A Second Selection, *K Richardson*
Sunderland, *S Miller & B Bell*
Teesdale, *D Coggins*
Teesdale: A Second Selection, *P Raine*
Weardale, *J Crosby*
Weardale: A Second Selection, *J Crosby*

DYFED

Aberystwyth and North Ceredigion,
  Dyfed Cultural Services Dept
Haverfordwest, *Dyfed Cultural Services Dept*
Upper Tywi Valley, *Dyfed Cultural Services Dept*

ESSEX

Around Grays, *B Evans*

GLOUCESTERSHIRE

Along the Avon from Stratford to Tewkesbury, *J Jeremiah*
Cheltenham: A Second Selection, *R Whiting*
Cheltenham at War, *P Gill*
Cirencester, *J Welsford*
Around Cirencester, *E Cuss & P Griffiths*
Forest, The, *D Mullin*
Gloucester, *J Voyce*
Around Gloucester, *A Sutton*
Gloucester: From the Walwin Collection, *J Voyce*
North Cotswolds, *D Viner*
Severn Vale, *A Sutton*
Stonehouse to Painswick, *A Sutton*
Stroud and the Five Valleys, *S Gardiner & L Padin*
Stroud and the Five Valleys: A Second Selection,
  S Gardiner & L Padin
Stroud's Golden Valley, *S Gardiner & L Padin*
Stroudwater and Thames & Severn Canals,
  E Cuss & S Gardiner
Stroudwater and Thames & Severn Canals: A Second
  Selection, *E Cuss & S Gardiner*
Tewkesbury and the Vale of Gloucester, *C Hilton*
Thornbury to Berkeley, *J Hudson*
Uley, Dursley and Cam, *A Sutton*
Wotton-under-Edge to Chipping Sodbury, *A Sutton*

GWYNEDD

Anglesey, *M Hitches*
Gwynedd Railways, *M Hitches*
Around Llandudno, *M Hitches*
Vale of Conwy, *M Hitches*

HAMPSHIRE

Gosport, *J Sadden*
Portsmouth, *P Rogers & D Francis*

HEREFORDSHIRE

Herefordshire, *A Sandford*

HERTFORDSHIRE

Barnet, *I Norrie*
Hitchin, *A Fleck*
St Albans, *S Mullins*
Stevenage, *M Appleton*

ISLE OF MAN

The Tourist Trophy, *B Snelling*

ISLE OF WIGHT

Newport, *D Parr*
Around Ryde, *D Parr*

JERSEY

Jersey: A Third Selection, *R Lemprière*

KENT

Bexley, *M Scott*
Broadstairs and St Peter's, *J Whyman*
Bromley, Keston and Hayes, *M Scott*
Canterbury: A Second Selection, *D Butler*
Chatham and Gillingham, *P MacDougall*
Chatham Dockyard, *P MacDougall*
Deal, *J Broady*
Early Broadstairs and St Peter's, *B Wootton*
East Kent at War, *D Collyer*
Eltham, *J Kennett*
Folkestone: A Second Selection, *A Taylor & E Rooney*
Goudhurst to Tenterden, *A Guilmant*
Gravesend, *R Hiscock*
Around Gravesend, *R Hiscock & D Grierson*
Herne Bay, *J Hawkins*
Lympne Airport, *D Collyer*
Maidstone, *I Hales*
Margate, *R Clements*
RAF Hawkinge, *R Humphreys*
RAF Manston, *RAF Manston History Club*
RAF Manston: A Second Selection,
  RAF Manston History Club
Ramsgate and Thanet Life, *D Perkins*
Romney Marsh, *E Carpenter*
Sandwich, *C Wanostrocht*
Around Tonbridge, *C Bell*
Tunbridge Wells, *M Rowlands & I Beavis*
Tunbridge Wells: A Second Selection,
  M Rowlands & I Beavis
Around Whitstable, *C Court*
Wingham, Adisham and Littlebourne, *M Crane*

LANCASHIRE

Around Barrow-in-Furness, *J Garbutt & J Marsh*
Blackpool, *C Rothwell*
Bury, *J Hudson*
Chorley and District, *J Smith*
Fleetwood, *C Rothwell*
Heywood, *J Hudson*
Around Kirkham, *C Rothwell*
Lancashire North of the Sands, *J Garbutt & J Marsh*
Around Lancaster, *S Ashworth*
Lytham St Anne's, *C Rothwell*
North Fylde, *C Rothwell*
Radcliffe, *J Hudson*
Rossendale, *B Moore & N Dunnachie*

LEICESTERSHIRE

Around Ashby-de-la-Zouch, *K Hillier*
Charnwood Forest, *I Keil, W Humphrey & D Wix*
Leicester, *D Burton*
Leicester: A Second Selection, *D Burton*
Melton Mowbray, *T Hickman*
Around Melton Mowbray, *T Hickman*
River Soar, *D Wix, P Shacklock & I Keil*
Rutland, *T Clough*
Vale of Belvoir, *T Hickman*
Around the Welland Valley, *S Mastoris*

LINCOLNSHIRE

Grimsby, *J Tierney*
Around Grimsby, *J Tierney*
Grimsby Docks, *J Tierney*
Lincoln, *D Cuppleditch*